Stouffville Ontario Book 1 in Colour Photos, Saving Our History One Photo at a Time

Photography
by Barbara Raué
©2019

Series Name: Cruising Ontario

Book 221: Stouffville Book 1

Cover photo: 6 Albert Street, Page 57

©All the photos in this book have been taken with my cameras. I own the rights to them.

Series Name: Cruising Ontario
Saving Our History One Photo at a Time
in colour photos

Books Available in Alphabetical Order:
Aberfoyle, Acton, Ajax, Alton, Amherstburg, Ancaster, Arthur, Auburn, Aylmer, Ayr, Beaver Valley, Belgrave, Belleville, Bloomingdale, Blyth, Brantford, Brockville, Burford, Burlington, Caledon, Caledonia, Cambridge, Carlow, Chatsworth, Clifford, Collingwood, Conestogo, Delhi, Dorchester to Aylmer, Drayton, Drumbo, Dundas, Dunlop, Eden Mills, Elmira, Elora, Erin, Essex, Fergus, Goderich, Grimsby, Guelph, Hagersville, Hamilton, Hanover, Harriston, Hespeler, Jarvis, Kingston, Kingsville, Kitchener, Lake Superior, Lincoln, Linwood, Listowel, London, Lucknow, Merrickville, Mono, Mount Forest, Mount Pleasant, Neustadt, New Hamburg, Newboro, Newport, Niagara-on-the-Lake, Niagara Falls, North Bay, Oakville, Onondaga, Orangeville, Orillia, Oshawa, Owen Sound, Palmerston, Paris, Pelham, Perth, Peterborough, Petrolia, Pickering, Port Colborne, Port Elgin, Portland, Preston, Rockwood, Sarnia, Sault Ste. Marie, Seaforth, Sheffield, Shelburne, Simcoe, Smiths Falls, Smithville, Southampton, St. Catharines, St. George, St. Jacobs, St. Marys, St. Thomas, Stoney Creek, Stratford, Thamesford, Thunder Bay, Tillsonburg, Toronto, Waterdown, Waterford, Waterloo, Welland, Wellesley, West Flamborough, Westport, Whitby, Windsor, Wingham, Woodstock

Book 210: North Bay
Book 211: Fort Erie
Book 212-215 Haldimand County
Book 216: Sudbury
Book 217: Parry Sound
Book 218-219: Uxbridge
Book 220: Port Perry
Book 221: Stouffville

Table of Contents

Main Street	Page 5
Charles Street	Page 41
Rupert Avenue	Page 43
William Street	Page 49
Second Street	Page 51
Albert Street	Page 54

    Stouffville is the primary urban area within the town of Whitchurch–Stouffville. It is centered at the intersection of Main Street, Mill Street and Market Street.

    In 1805-06 Abraham Stouffer (1780-1851), a Pennsylvania Mennonite, bought four hundred acres of land in the area and built a saw and grist mill on Duffin's Creek and a settlement grew up around it. In 1832 a post office named Stouffville was established. By 1864, with a population of about seven hundred, there were several prosperous industries including carriage works, harness works, and the mills of Edward Wheler, a prominent merchant. The construction of the Toronto and Nipissing Railway was completed in 1871 and growing agricultural prosperity stimulated the community's growth.

A large number of the early settlers of present day Whitchurch-Stouffville were members of the Historic Peace Churches: Brethren in Christ (Tunkers), Mennonites, and Quakers. They were attracted to settle in Upper Canada by Lieutenant Governor John Graves Simcoe with the offer of military exemption (1793). The peace teachings of the Christian tradition greatly shaped their faith and caused them to wrestle with what it means to be people of God's peace, especially during times of conflict and war. As pioneers of conscientious objection in Canada, their commitment to the work of peace and reconciliation continues to stand witness in this community and around the world.

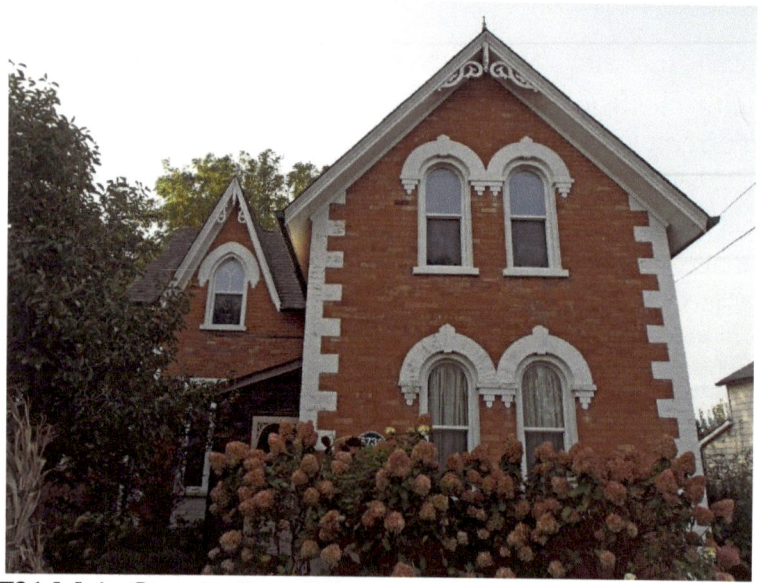

6731 Main Street – Late Victorian Hybrid – corner quoins, finials and trim on gables, voussoirs and keystones over windows

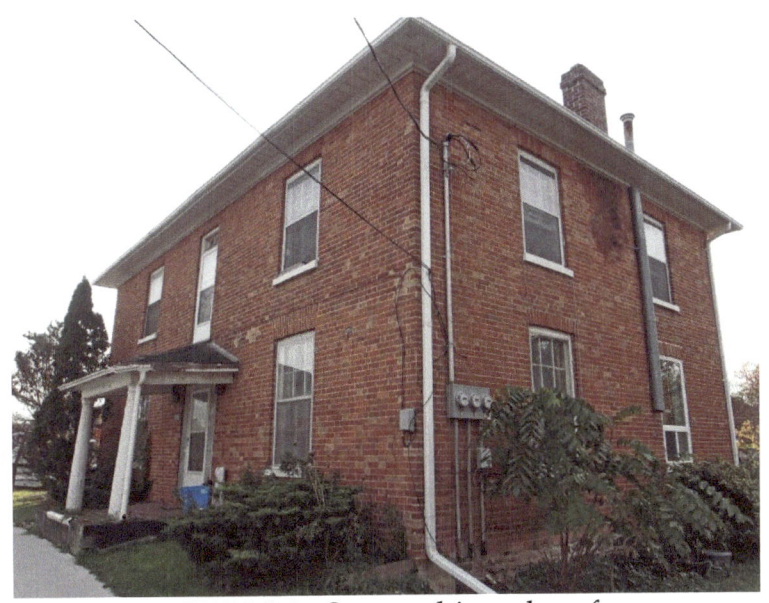

6745 Main Street – hipped roof

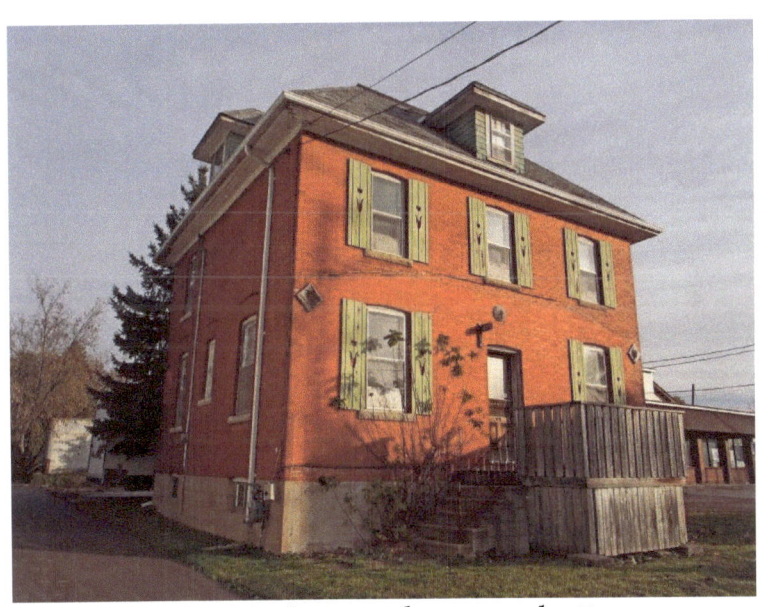

6718 Main Street – dormers, shutters

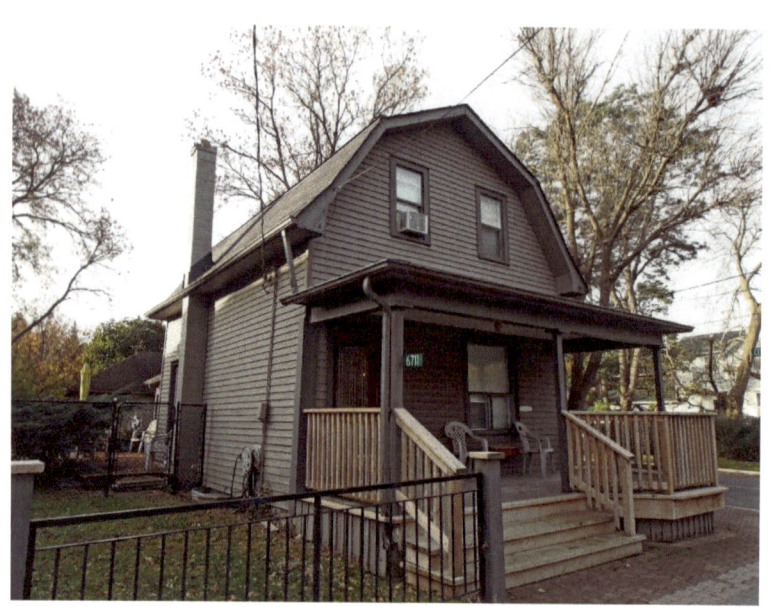

6711 Main Street – Neo-Colonial – gambrel roof

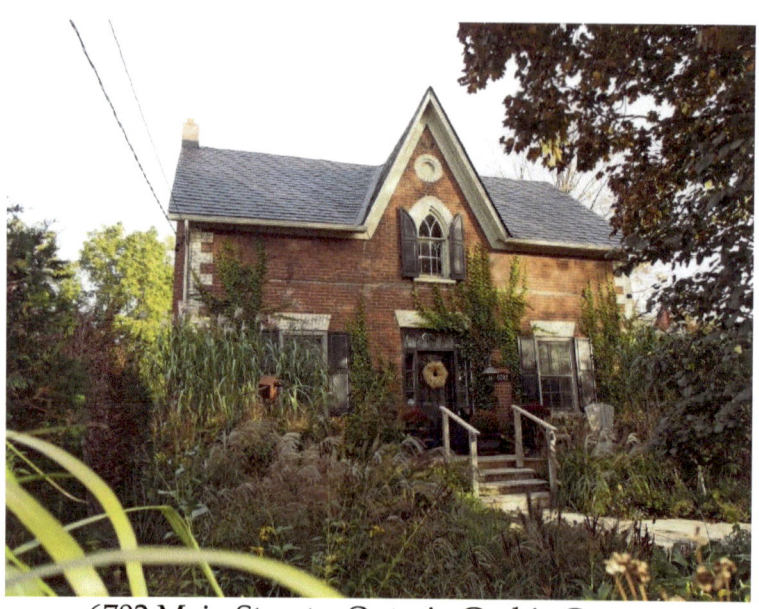

6702 Main Street – Ontario Gothic Cottage

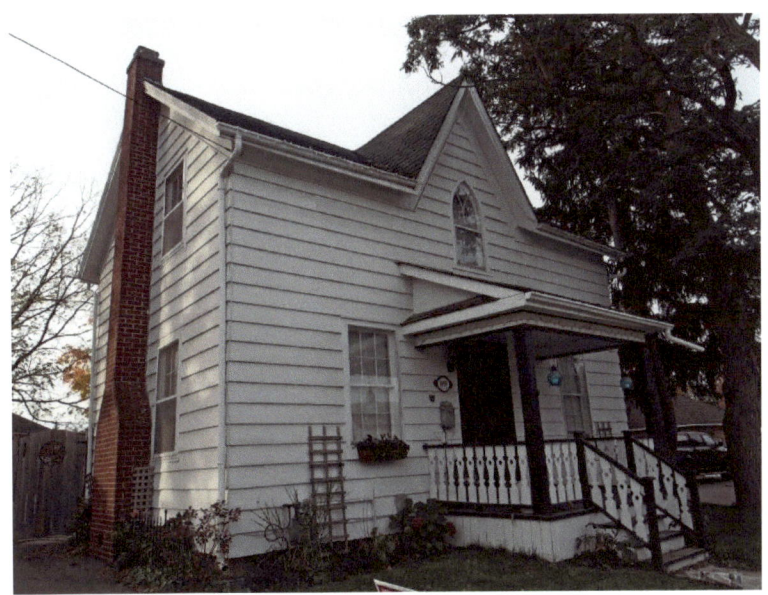

6699 Main Street – Gothic Revival

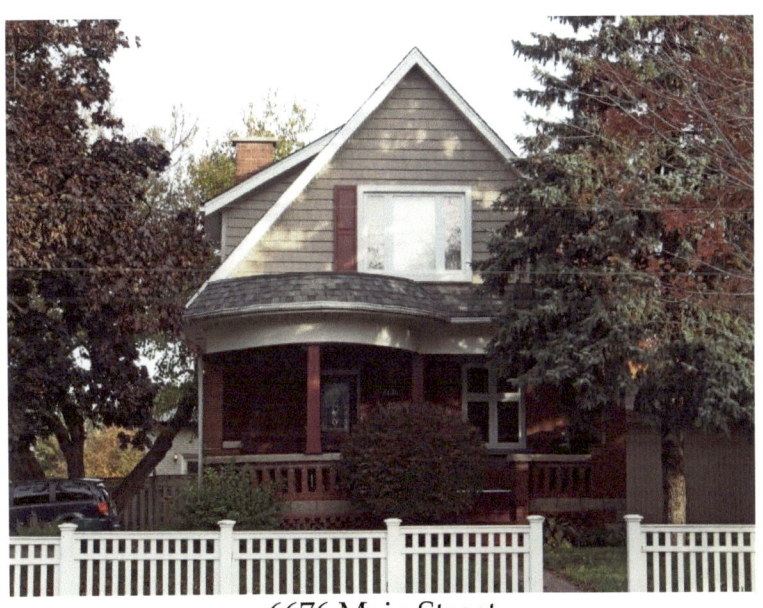

6676 Main Street

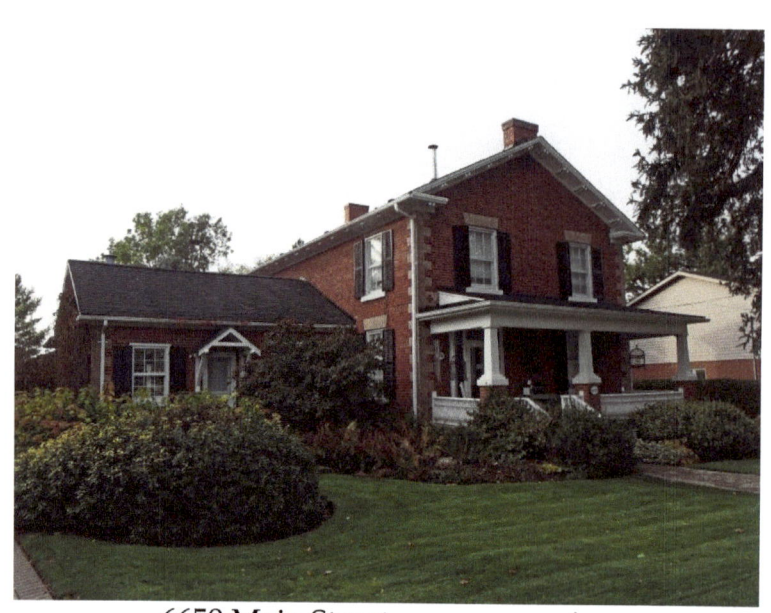

6659 Main Street – corner quoins

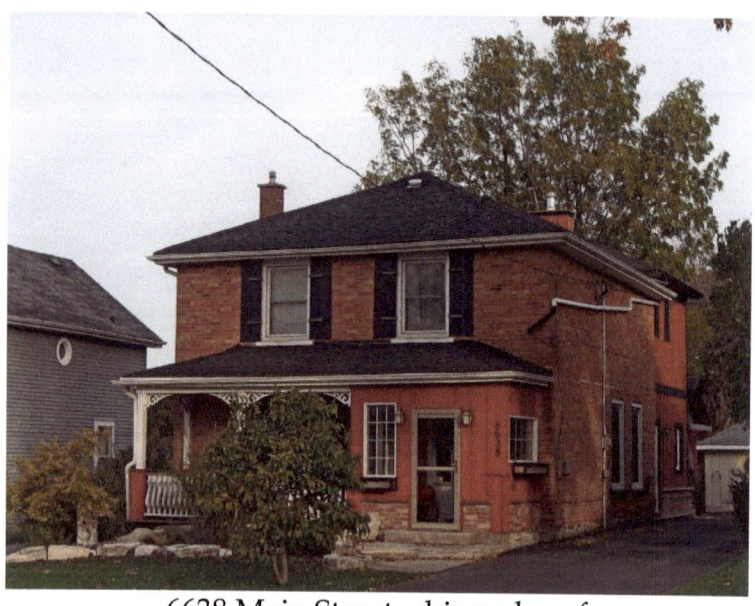

6638 Main Street – hipped roof

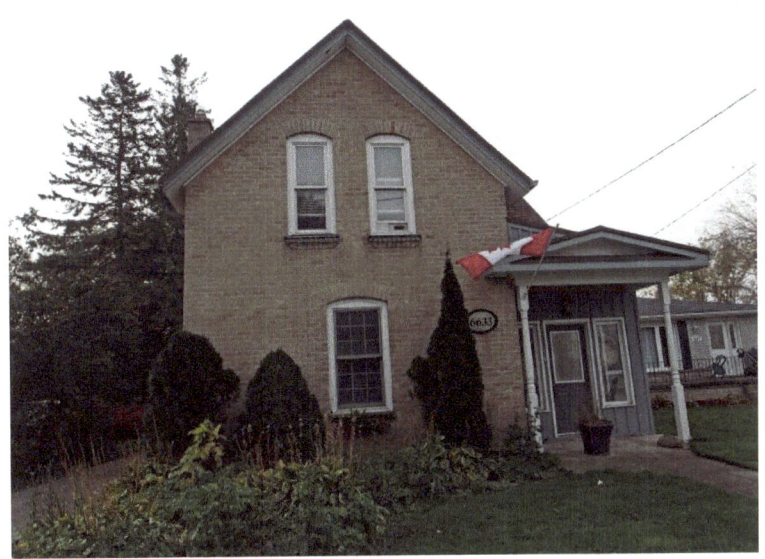

6633 Main Street

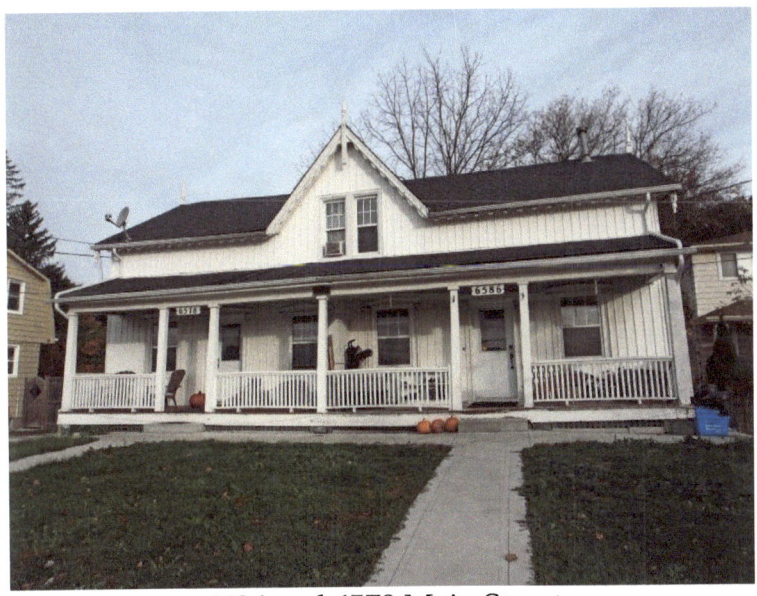

6586 and 6578 Main Street

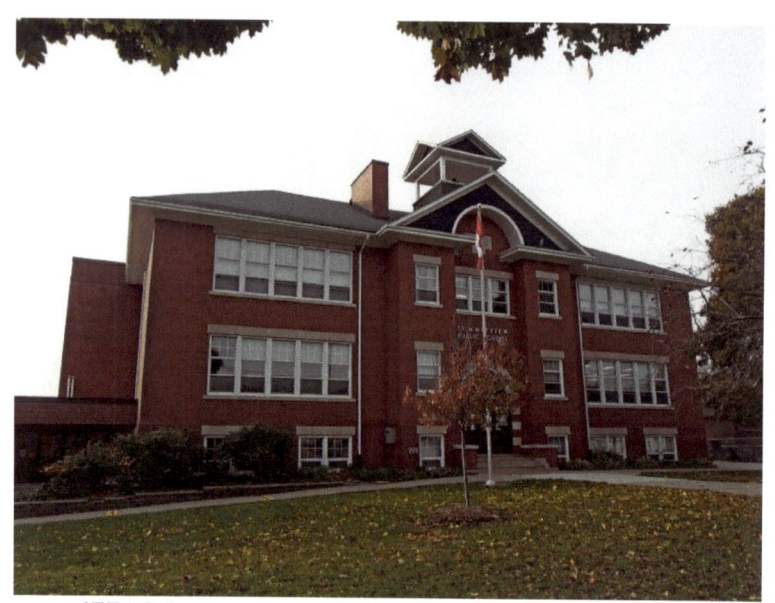

6551 Main Street - Summitview Public School

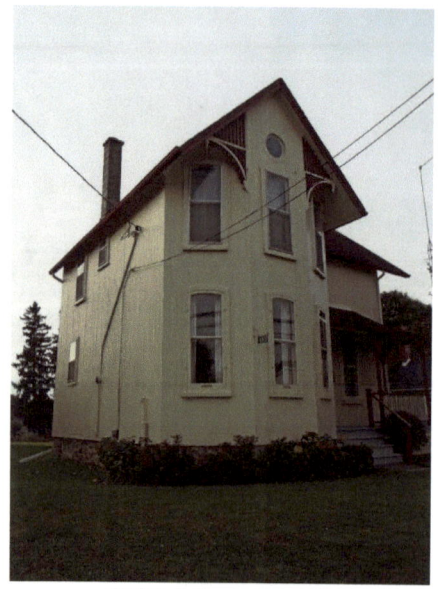

6531 Main Street

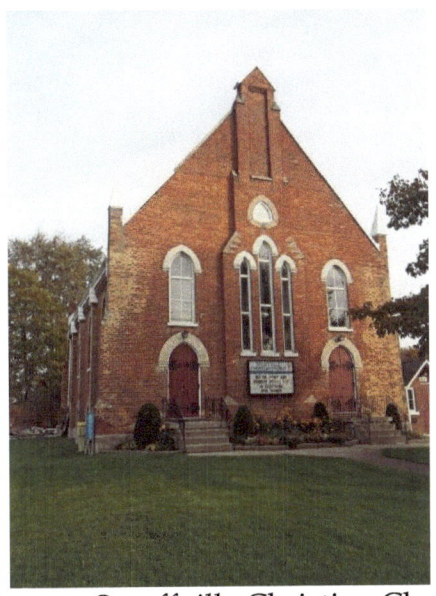

6528 Main Street – Stouffville Christian Church – Gothic Revival – lancet windows, buttresses with finials

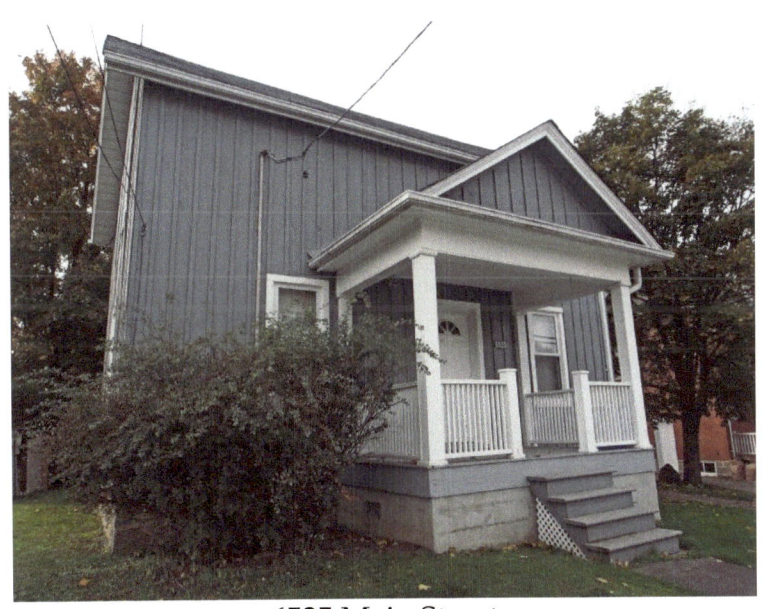

6525 Main Street

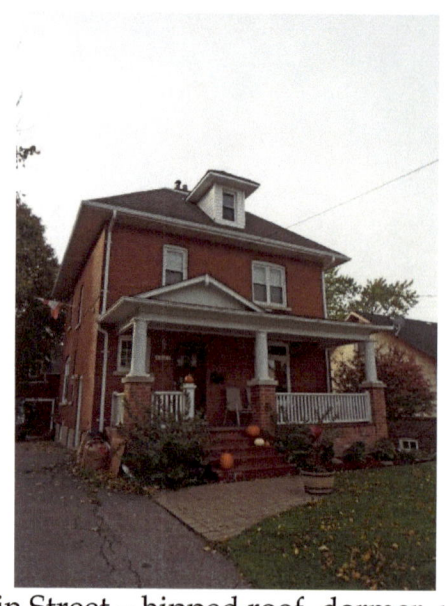

6521 Main Street – hipped roof, dormer, pediment

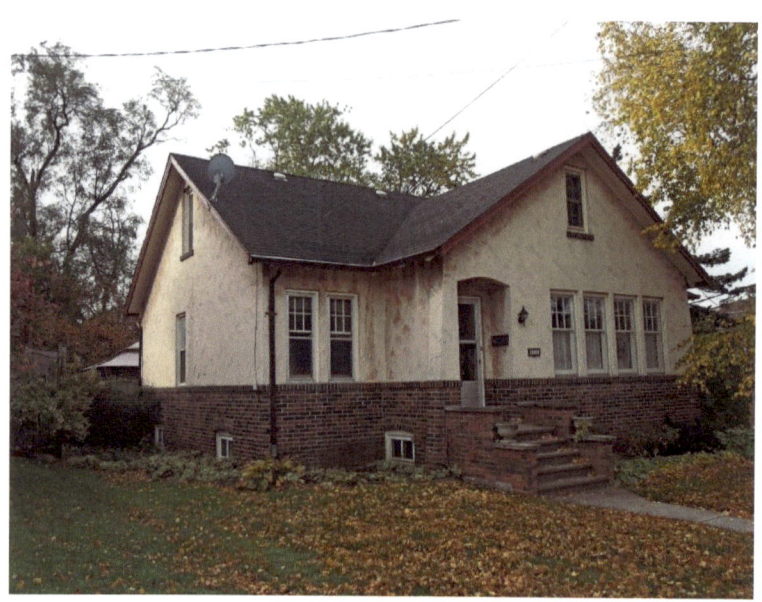

6511 Main Street

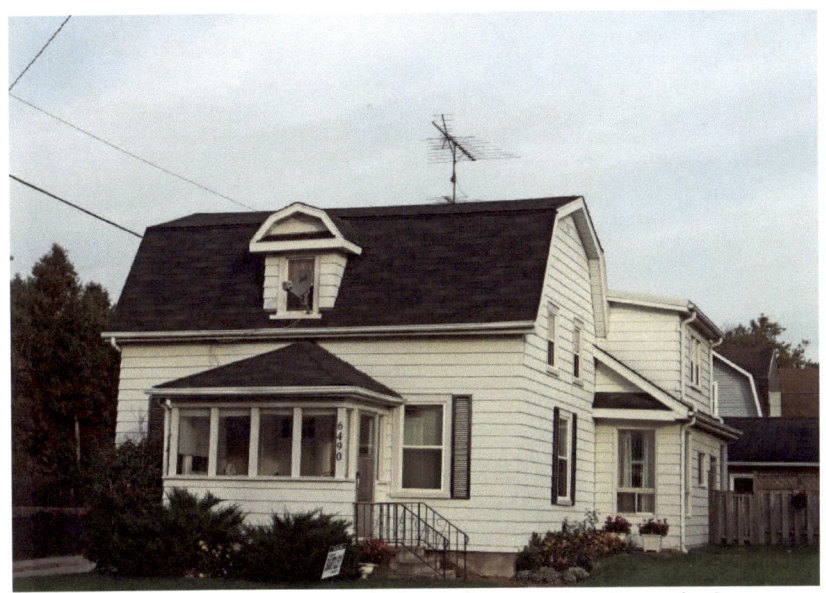

6490 Main Street – Neo-Colonial – gambrel roof, dormer

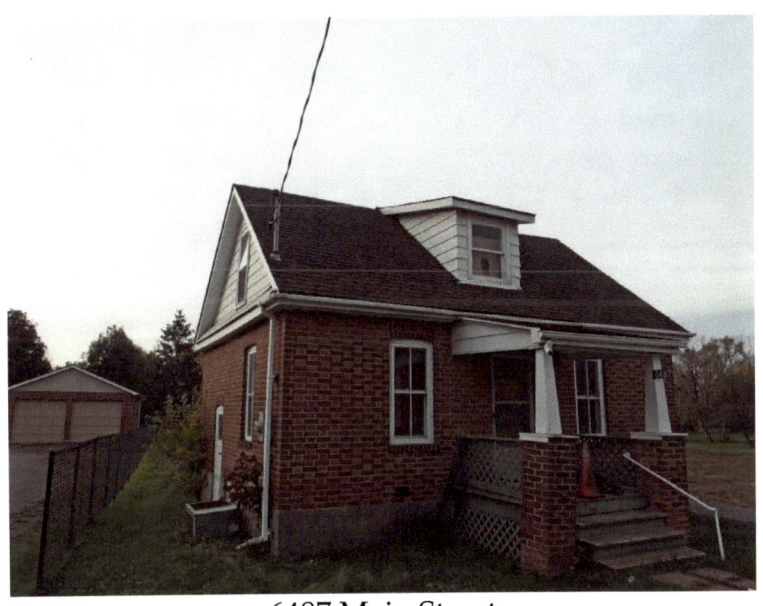

6487 Main Street

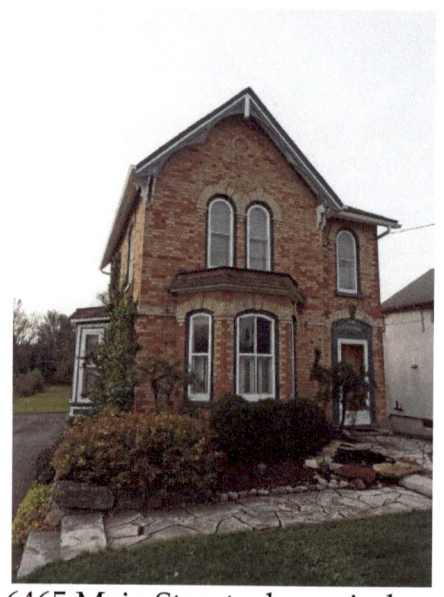
6465 Main Street – bay window

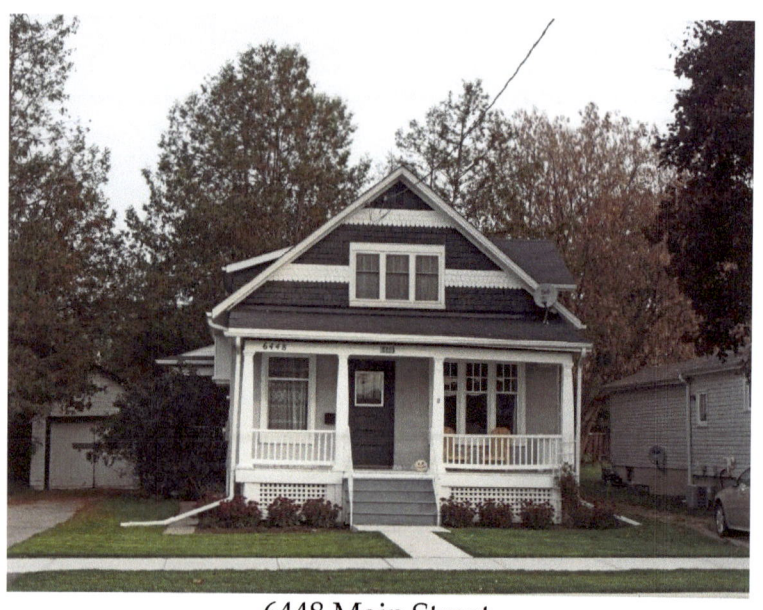
6448 Main Street

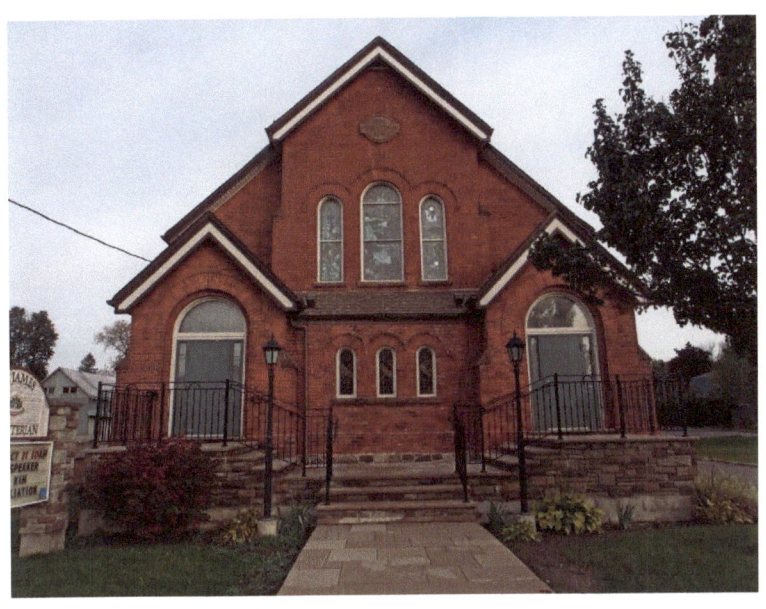

6432 Main Street – St. James Presbyterian Church

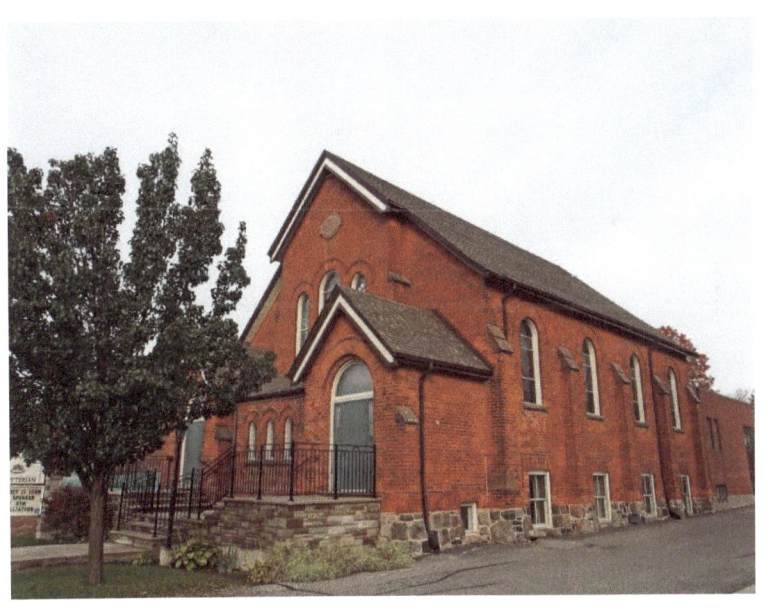

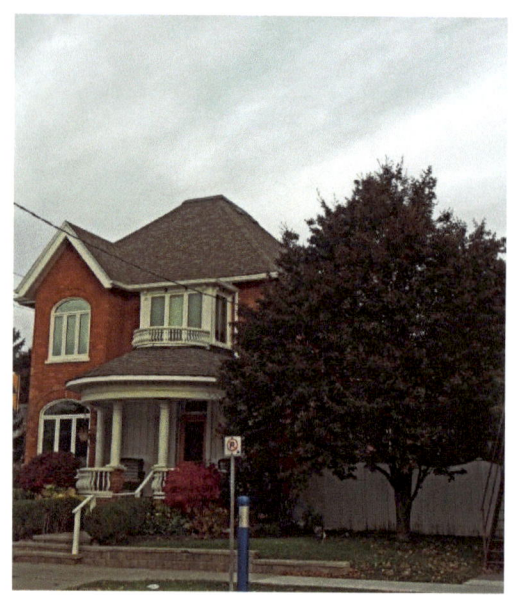

Main Street

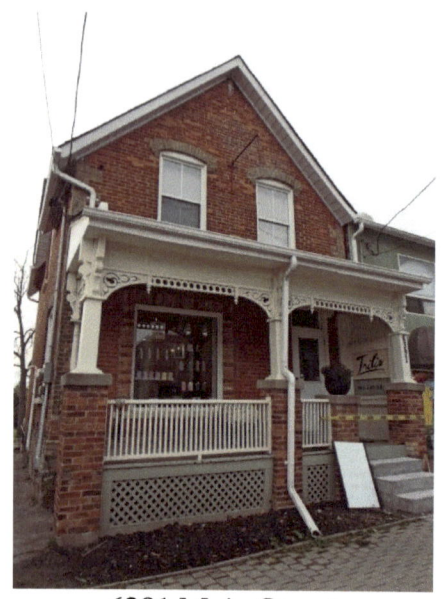

6391 Main Street

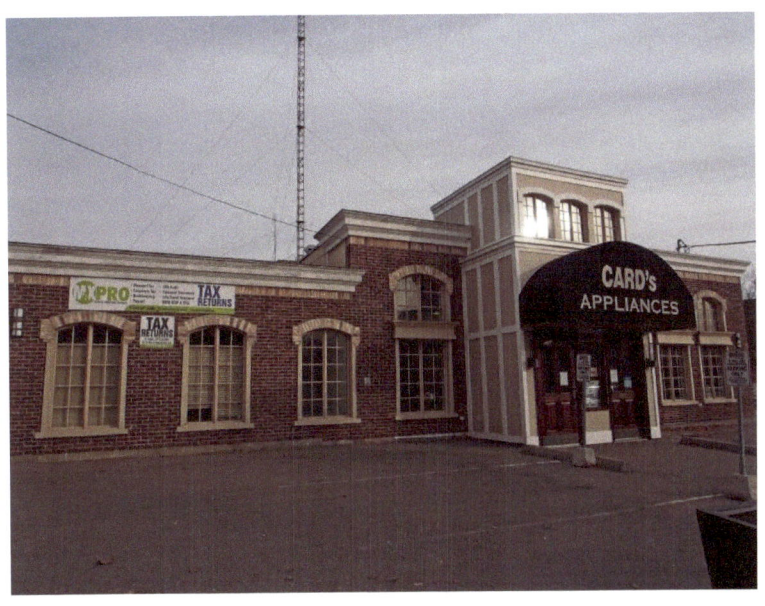

6392 Main Street

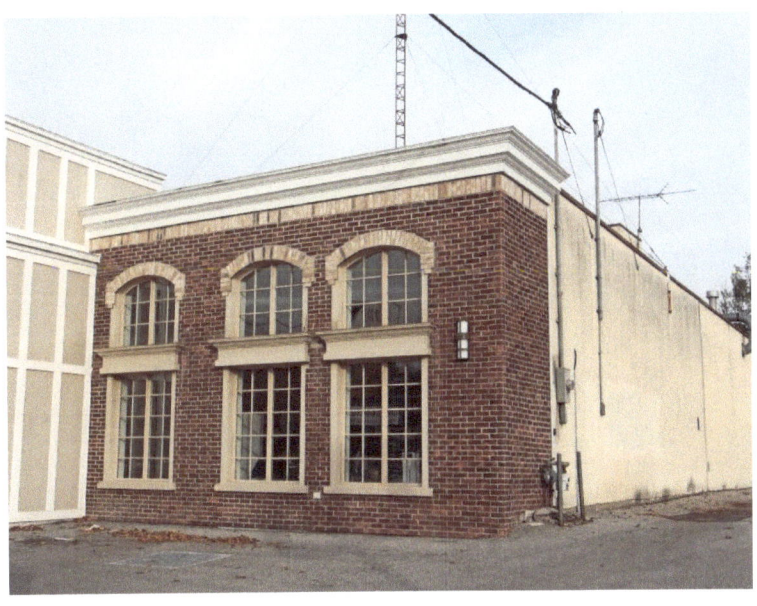

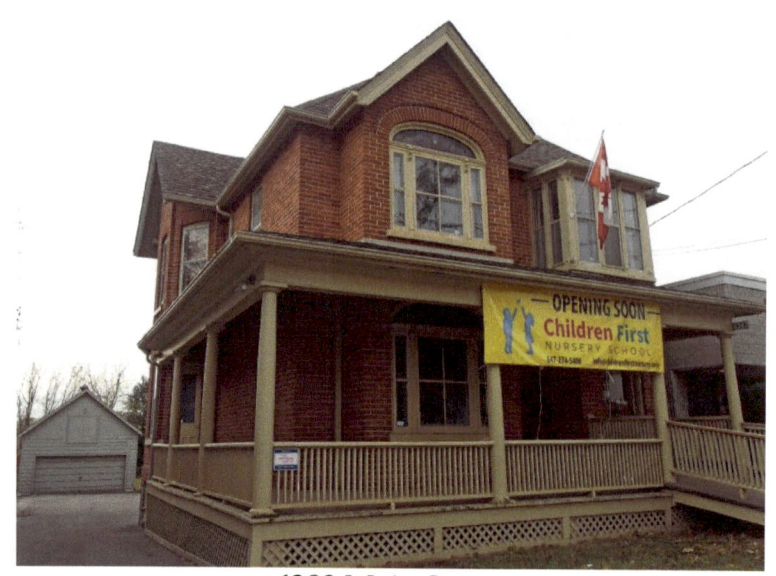

6383 Main Street

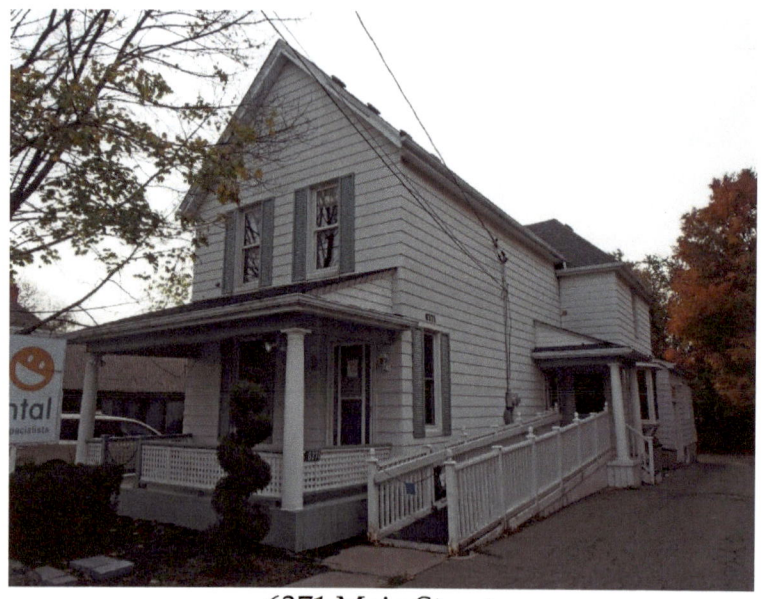

6371 Main Street

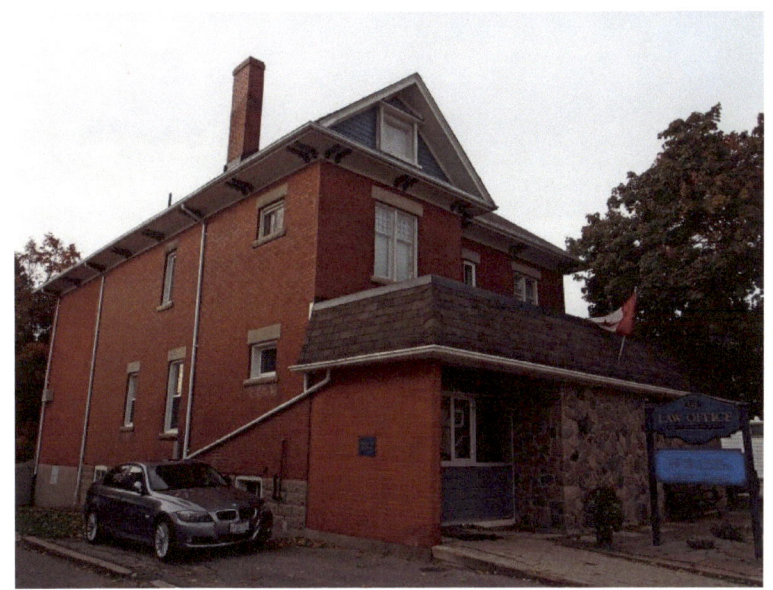

6361 Main Street

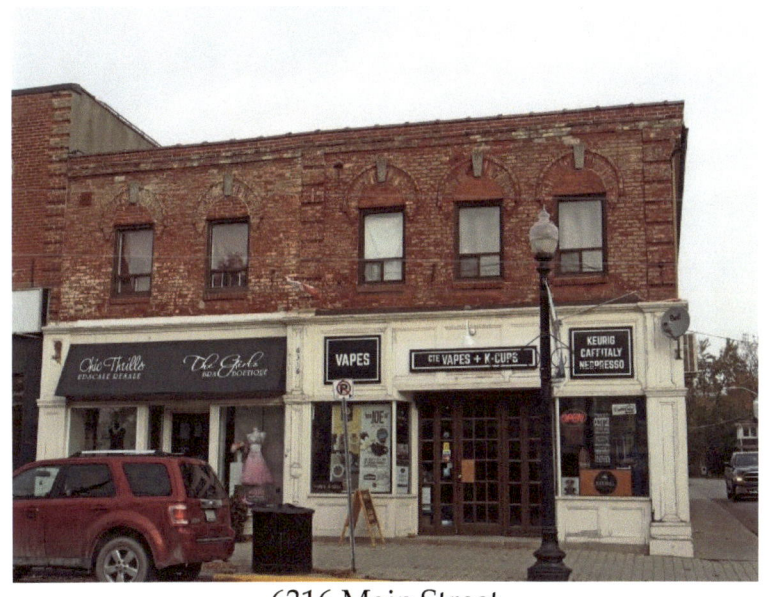

6316 Main Street

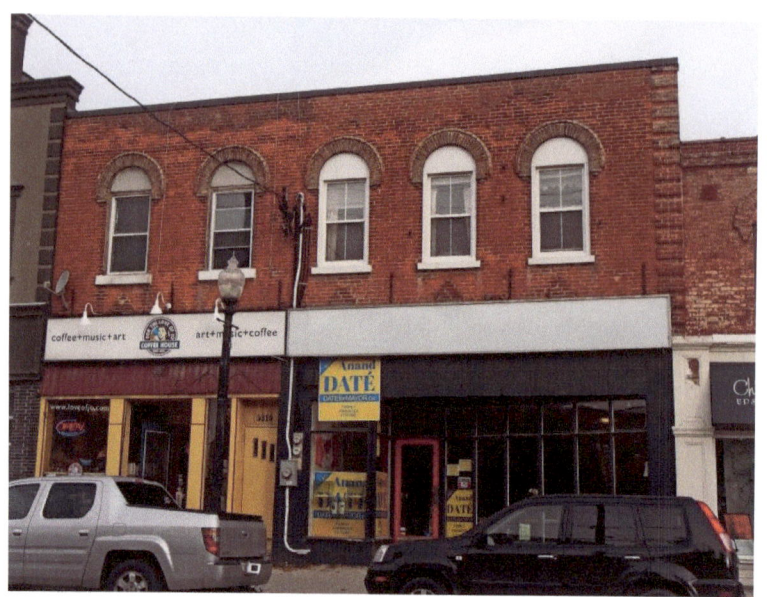
6310 Main Street

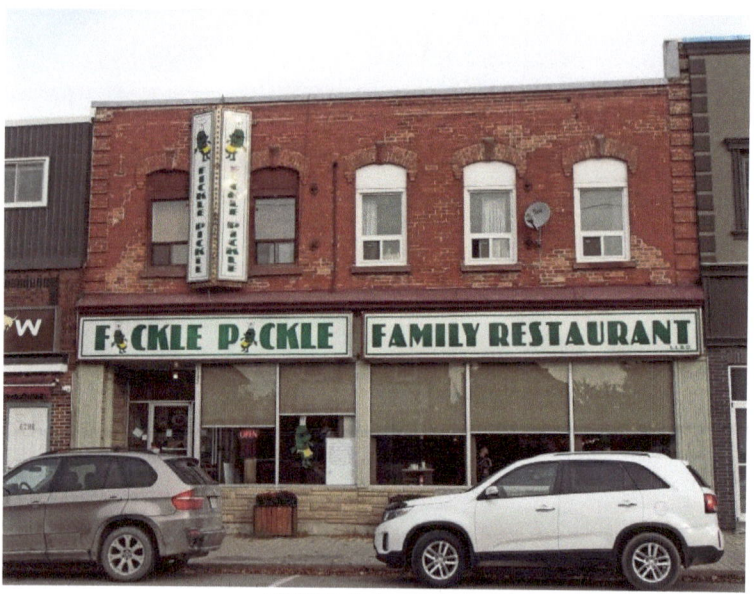
6302 Main Street

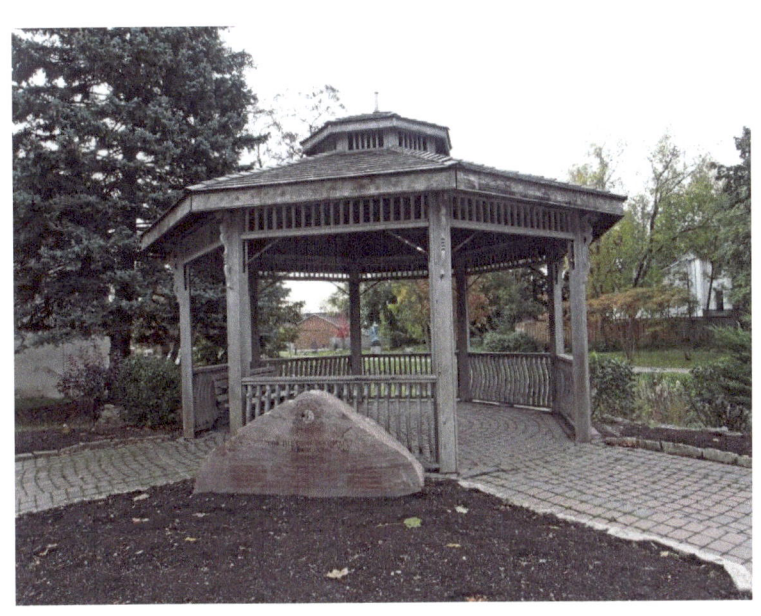

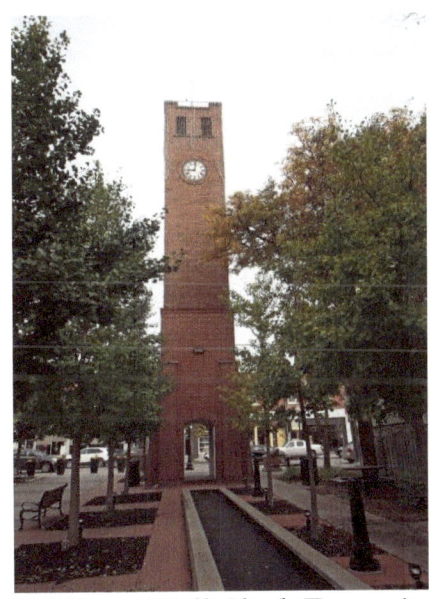

Main Street – Old Town Hall Clock Tower in Civic Square – 1931

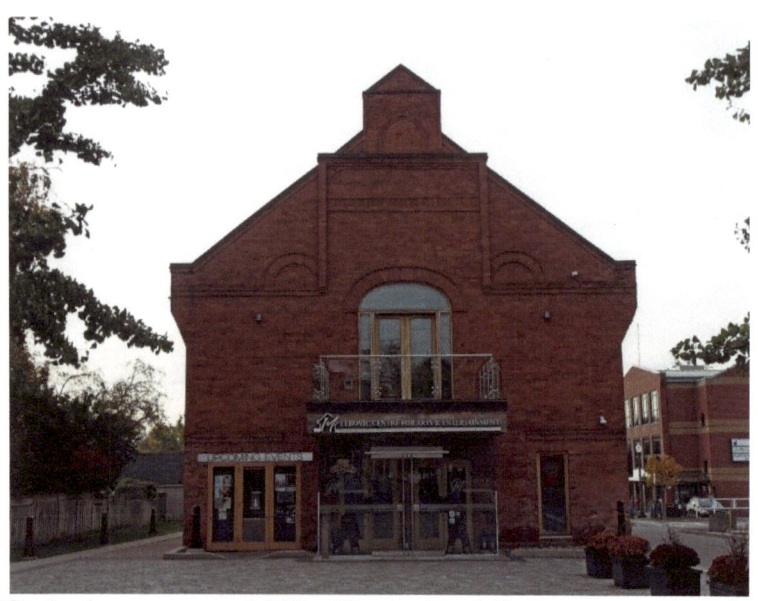

19 Civic Avenue – c. 1895 – Restrained Romanesque Revival - Originally a market/concert hall, it was later used as a movie theatre, bowling alley and billiard hall, garage before becoming Stouffville Town Hall and remained in use until the late 1990s -Lebovic Centre for Arts & Entertainment

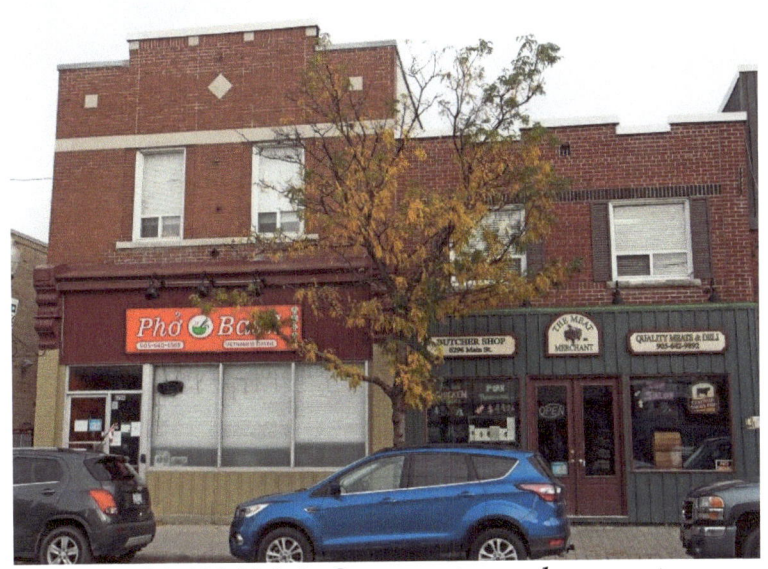

6294-6296 Main Street – stepped parapet

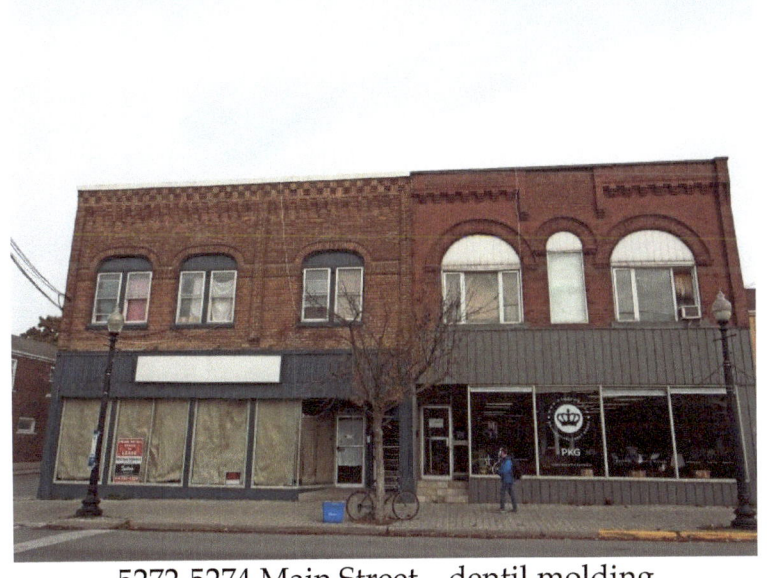

5272-5274 Main Street – dentil molding

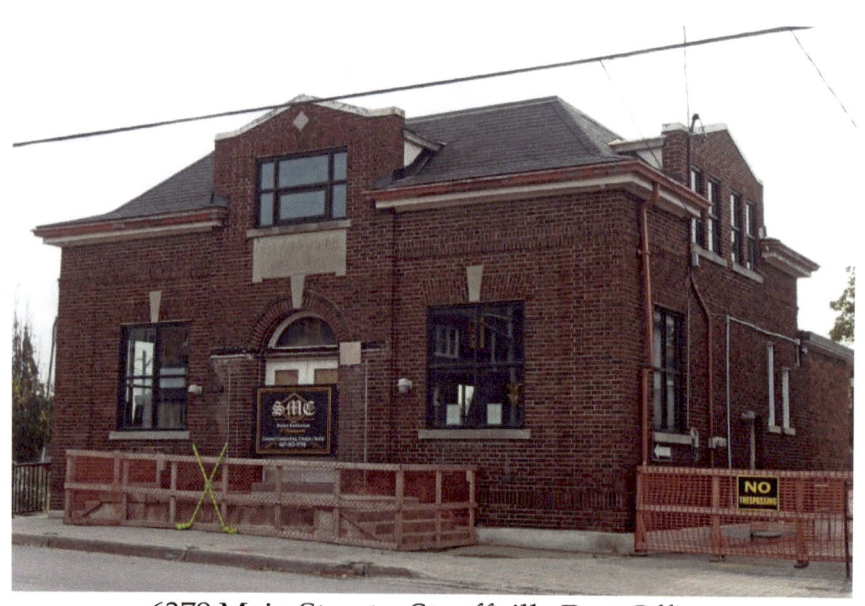

6379 Main Street – Stouffville Post Office

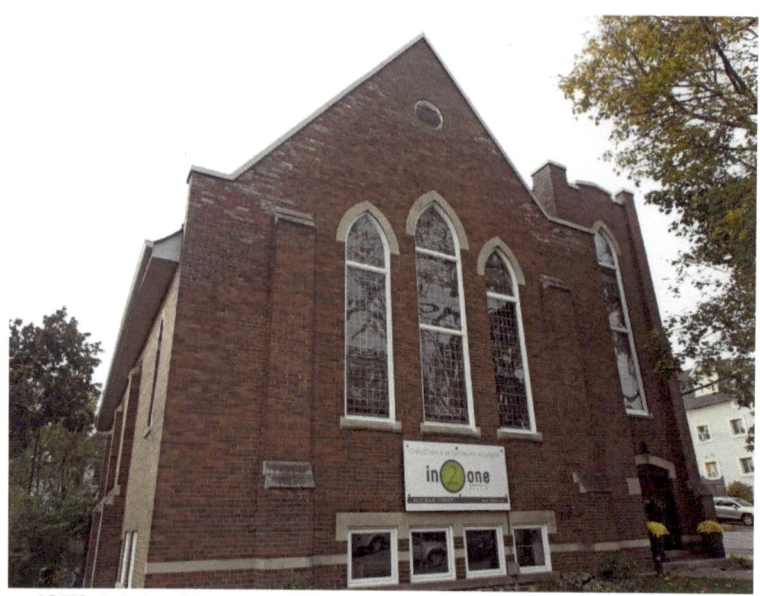

6273 Main Street – Christian & Missionary Alliance

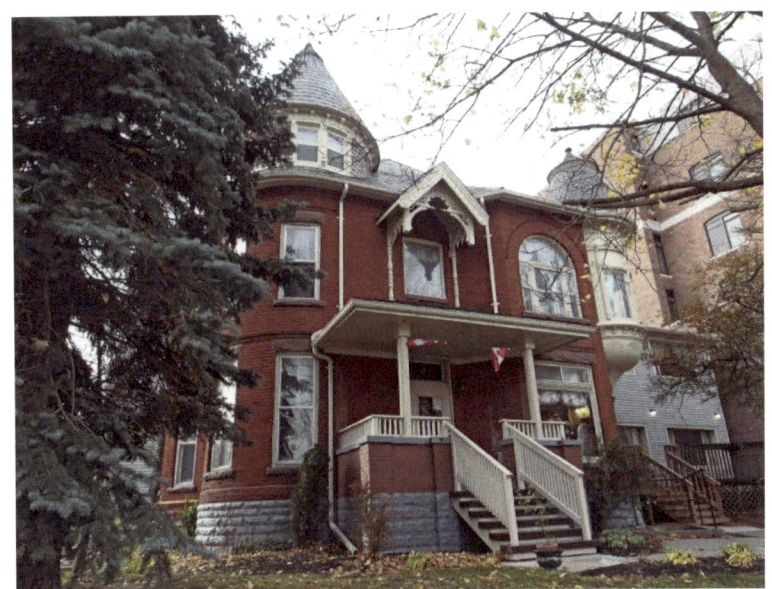

6257 Main Street – Buckingham Manor Retirement Living – three storey turret

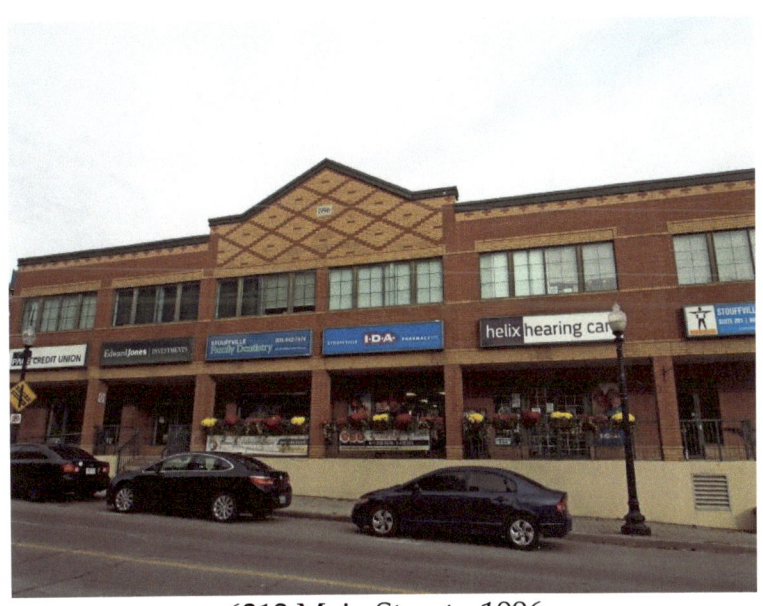

6212 Main Street - 1996

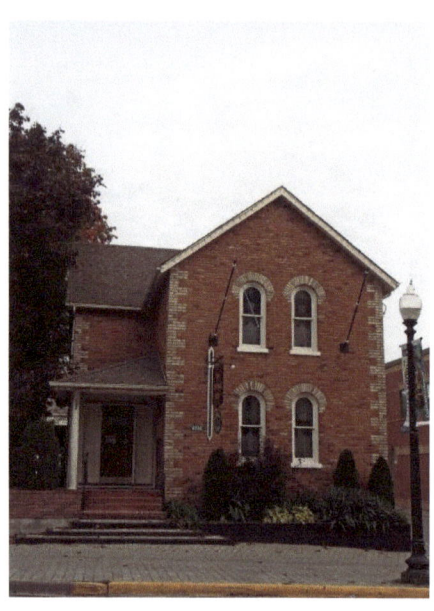

6204 Main Street – The Earl of Whitchurch Pub – corner quoins

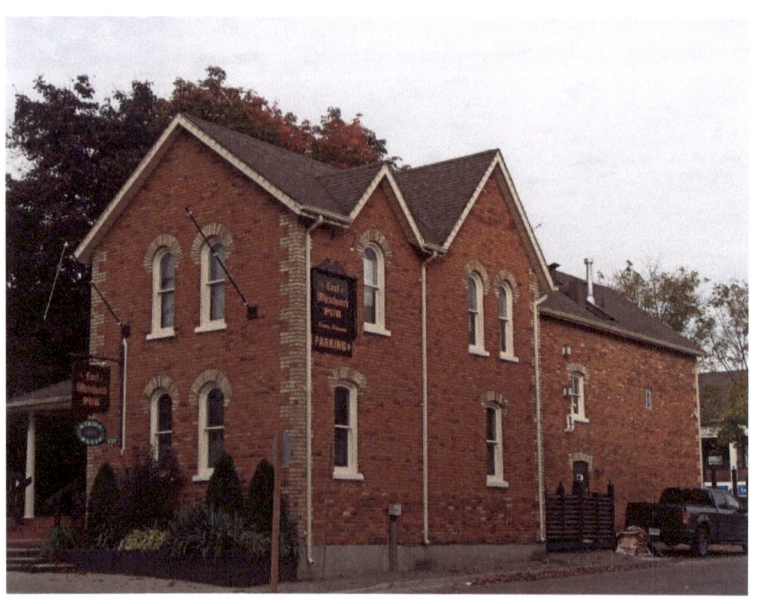

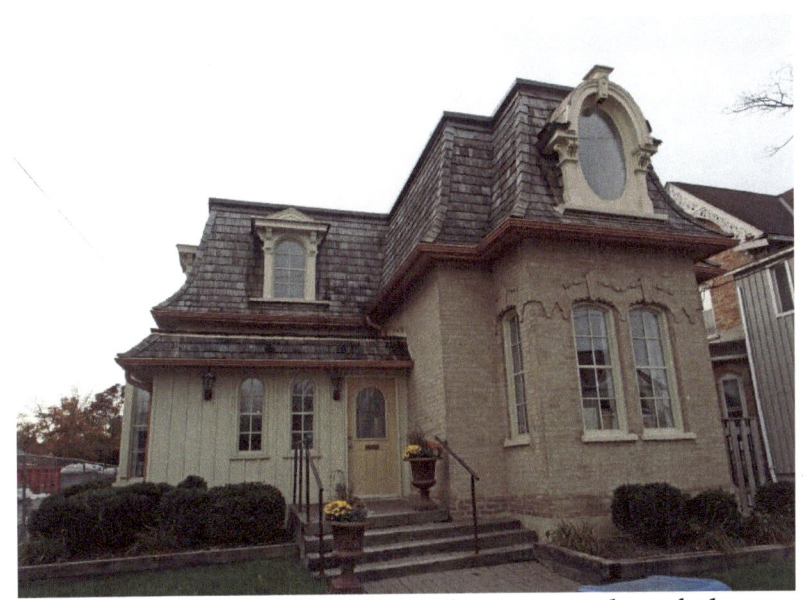

Main Street – Second Empire style - mansard roof, dormers with window hoods

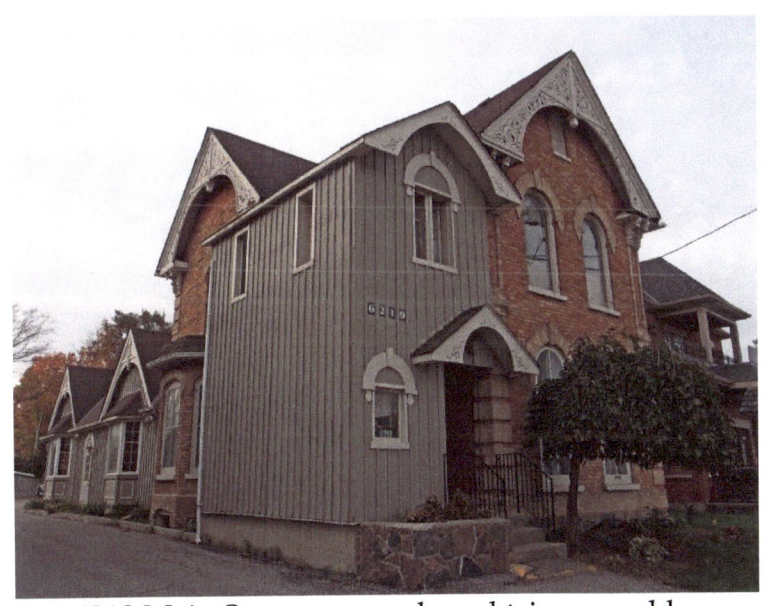

6219 Main Street – verge board trim on gables

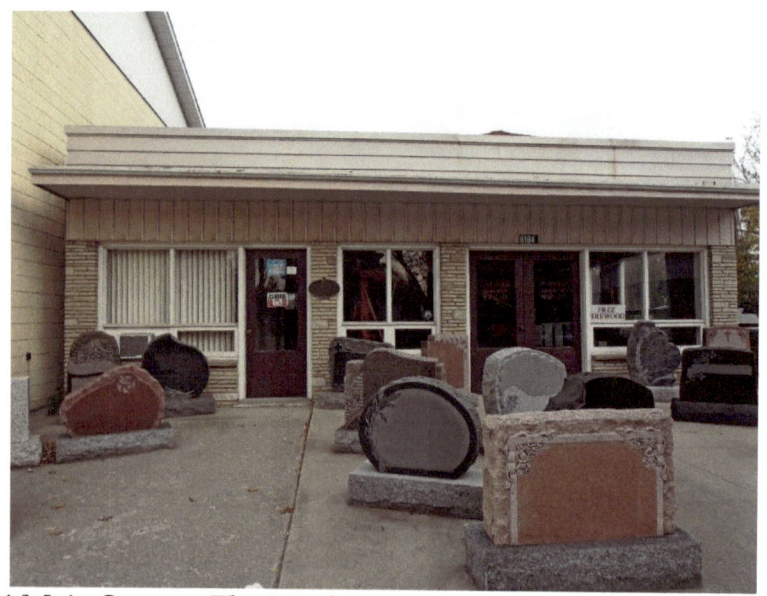

6194 Main Street – The Marble Works – Three generations of the Wideman family, Philip, son Ludwig, and grandson Bartholomew, operated a marble works first in Ringwood and then in Stouffville between 1839 and 1939. Ludwig moved the business to this site in 1885 and erected the shop portion of this building. The Tarr family, Percy and son Gordon, operated Stouffville Marble and Granite Works from 1939 to 1977. The Marks family, Vaughn and son Wayne, have operated the Stouffville Monument Works since 1978.

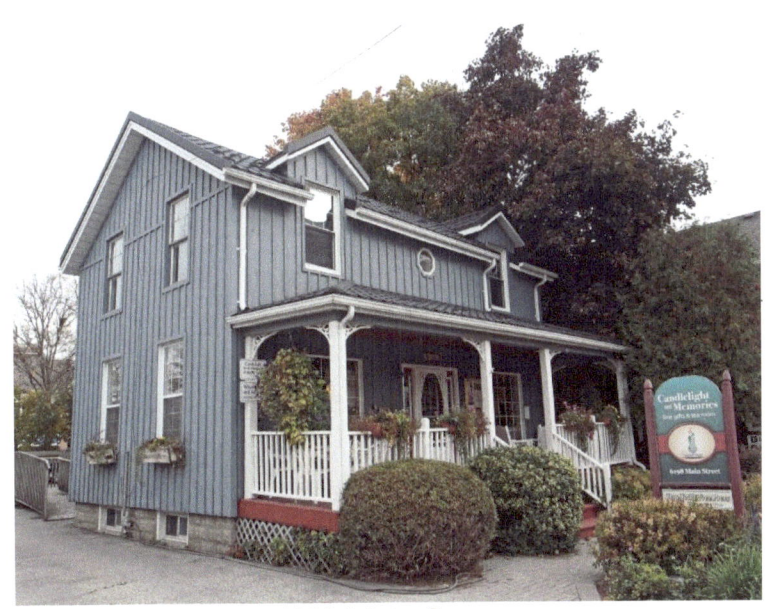

6198 Main Street

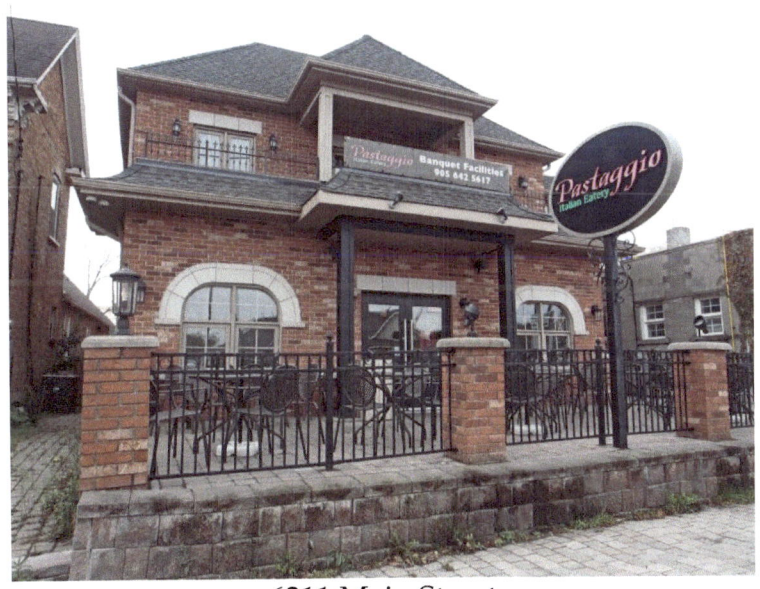

6211 Main Street

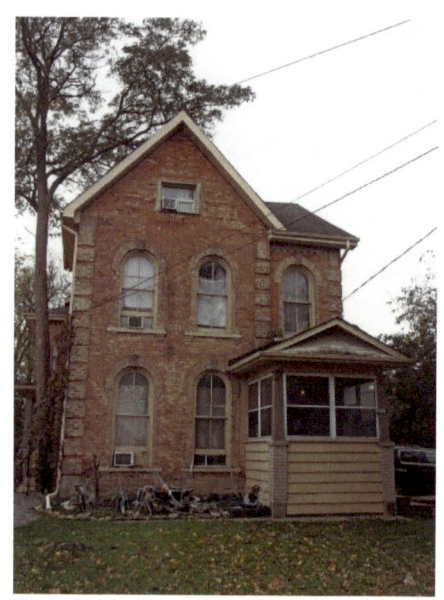

6185 Main Street – corner quoins

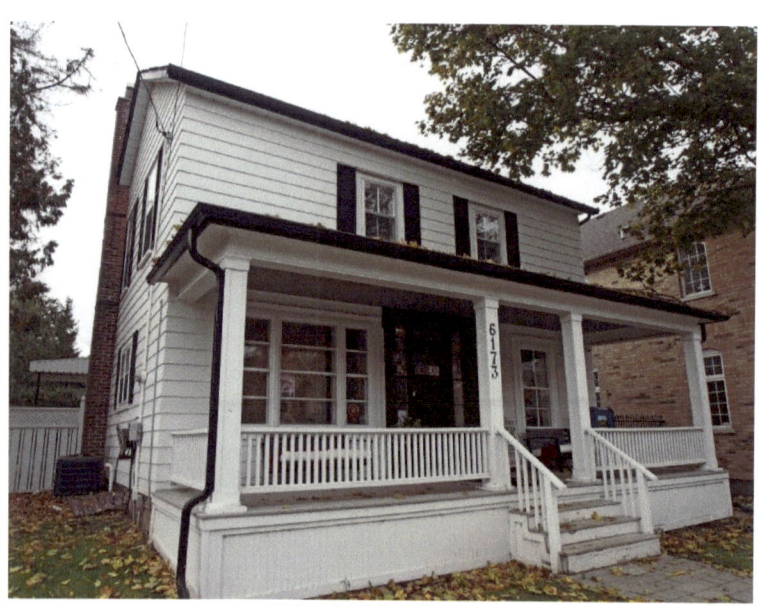

6173 Main Street

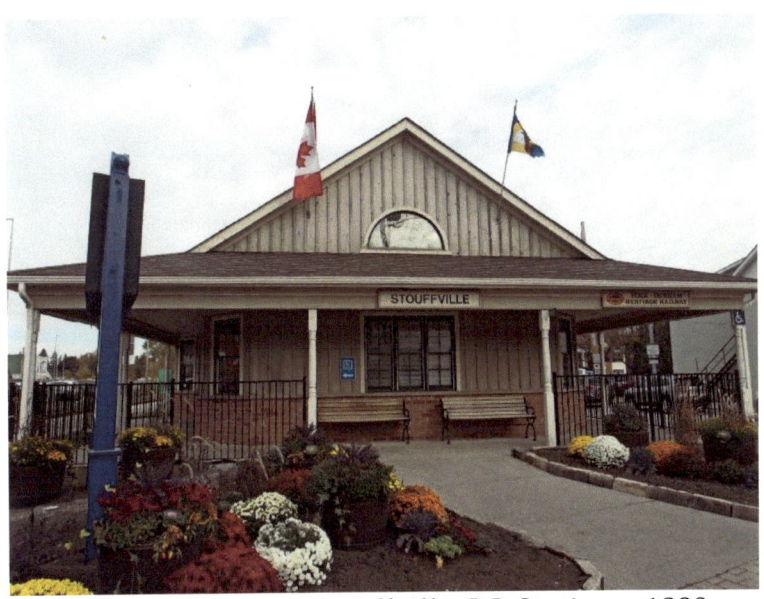

6176 Main Street – Stouffville GO Station – 1990s

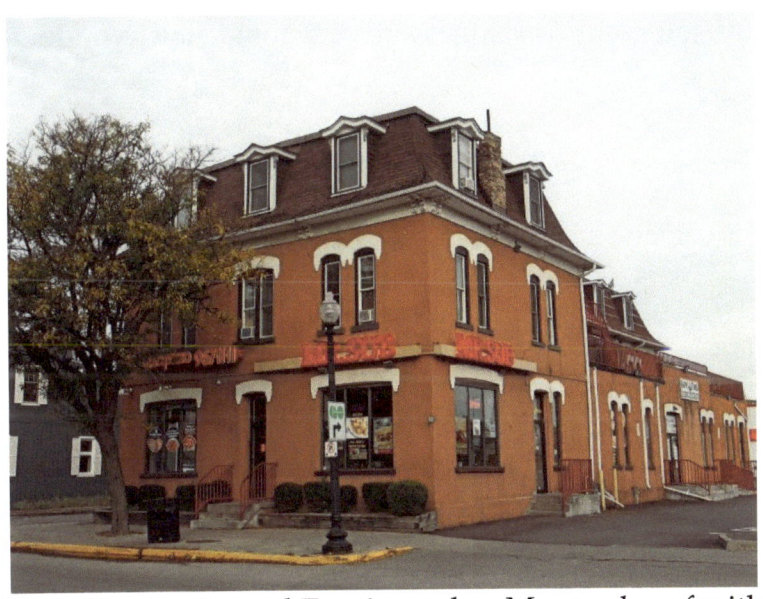

Main Street – Second Empire style – Mansard roof with dormers

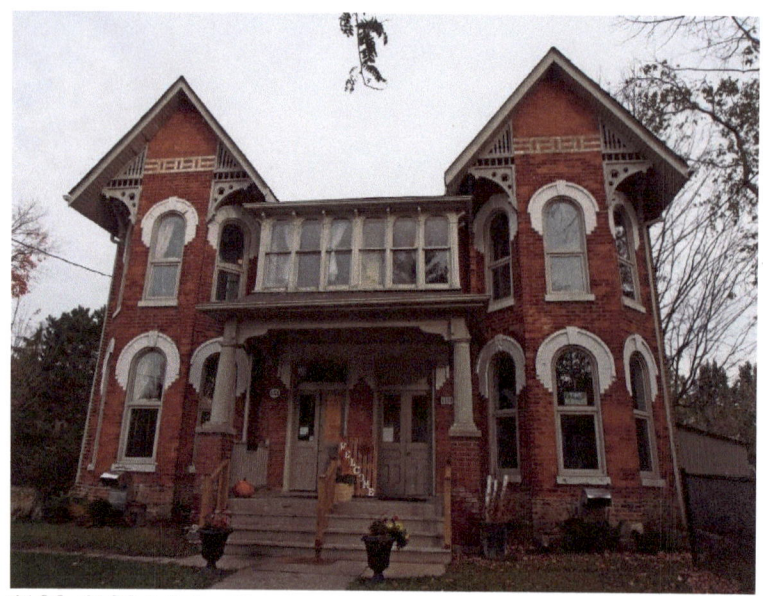

6128-6130 Main Street – two-storey towers flanking the entrance, fretwork, dichromatic brickwork, contrasting voussoirs with keystones and drip molds over windows

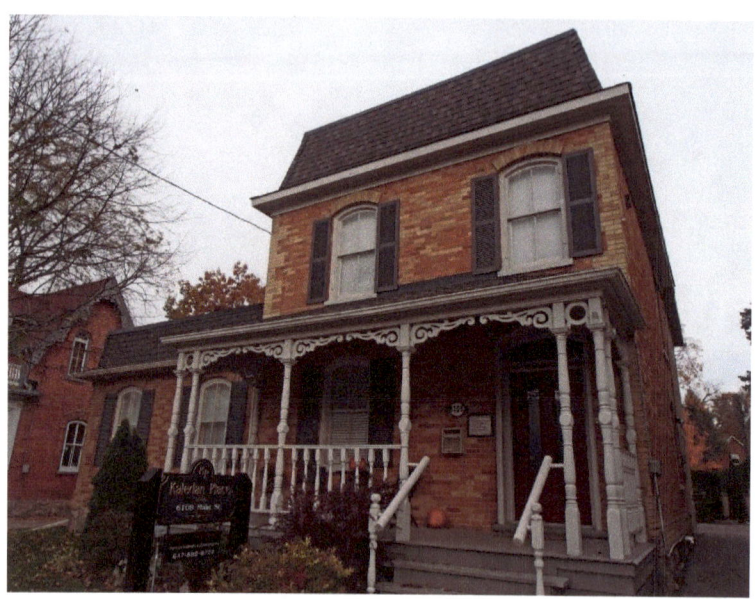

6108 Main Street

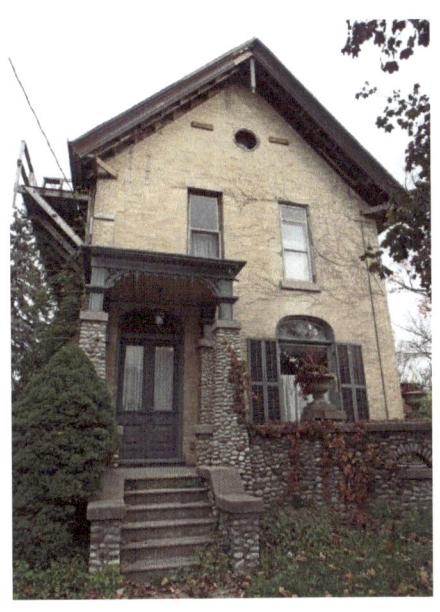

6120 Main Street – finials on gables, verge board trim, cobblestone veranda pillars, fretwork

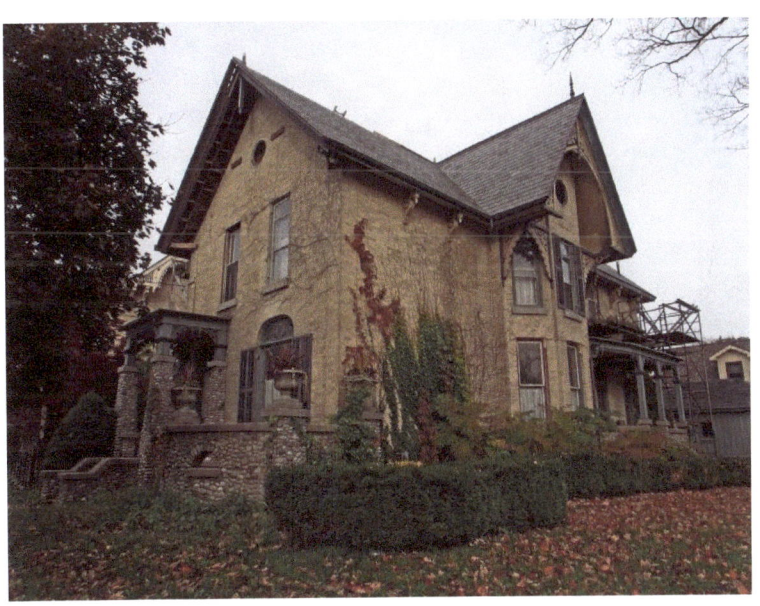

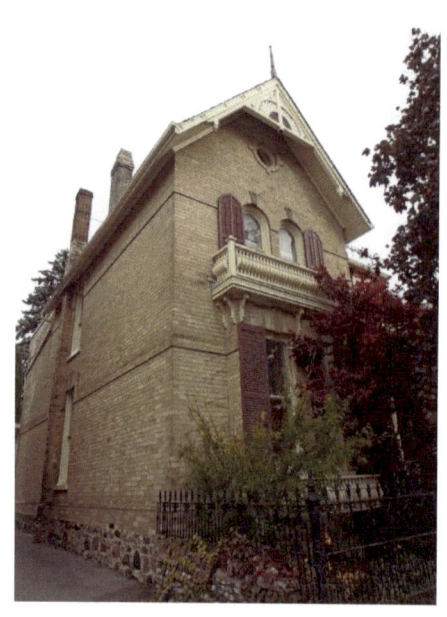

Main Street – verge board trim and finials on gables, balconies, cobblestone veranda and pillars

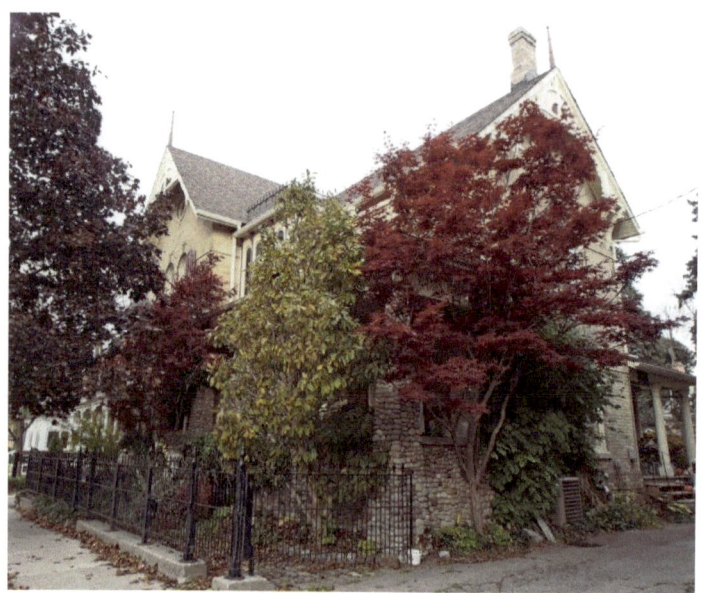

This angle shows the size of the house.

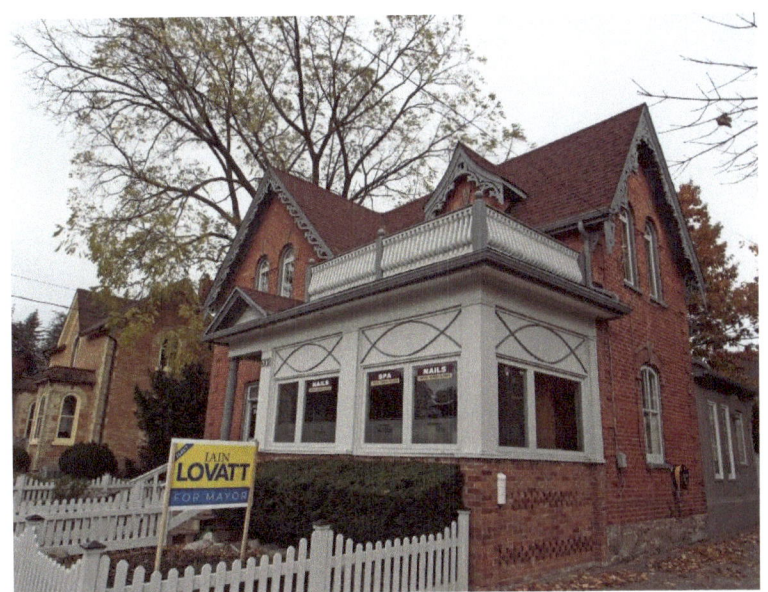

6102 Main Street

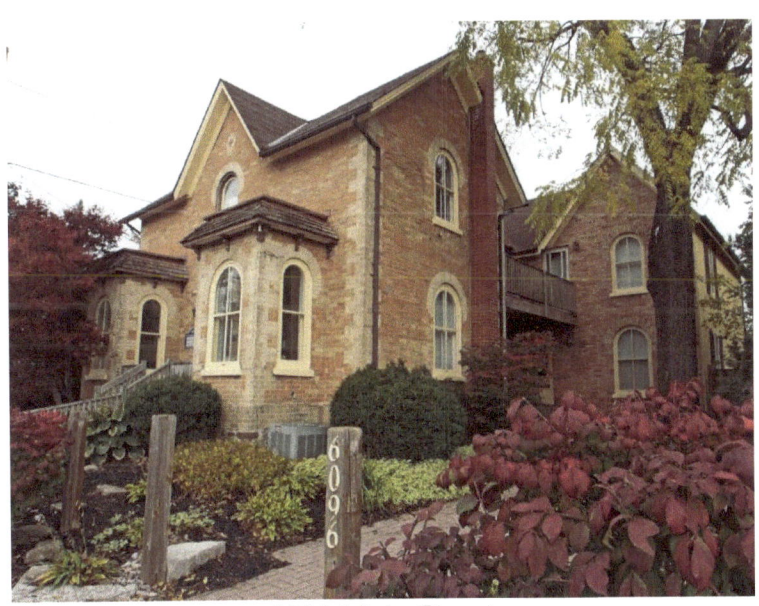

6096 Main Street

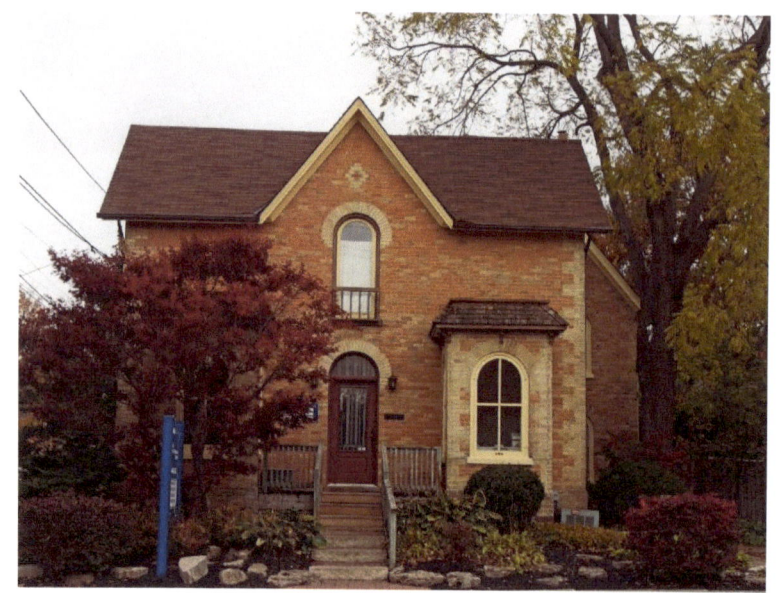

Main Street – Gothic Revival – corner quoins, bay window

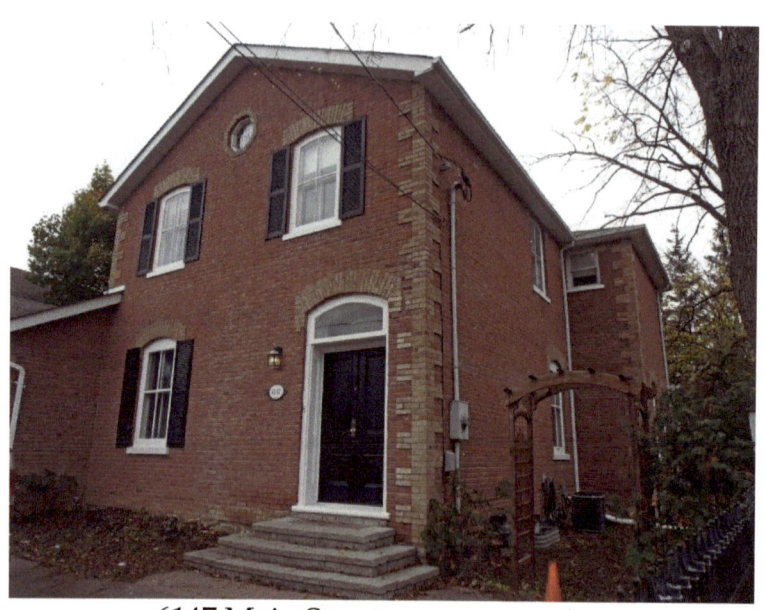

6147 Main Street – corner quoins

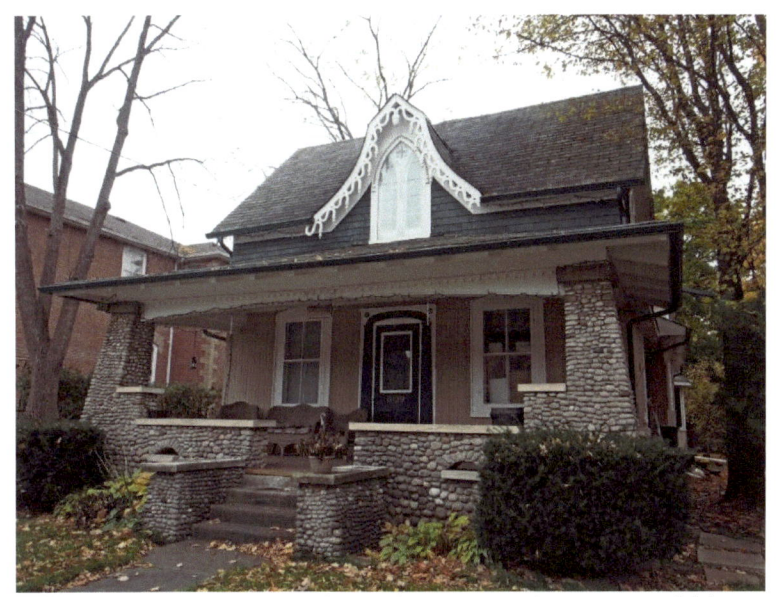

6139 Main Street – verge board trim on dormer, cobblestone veranda and pillars

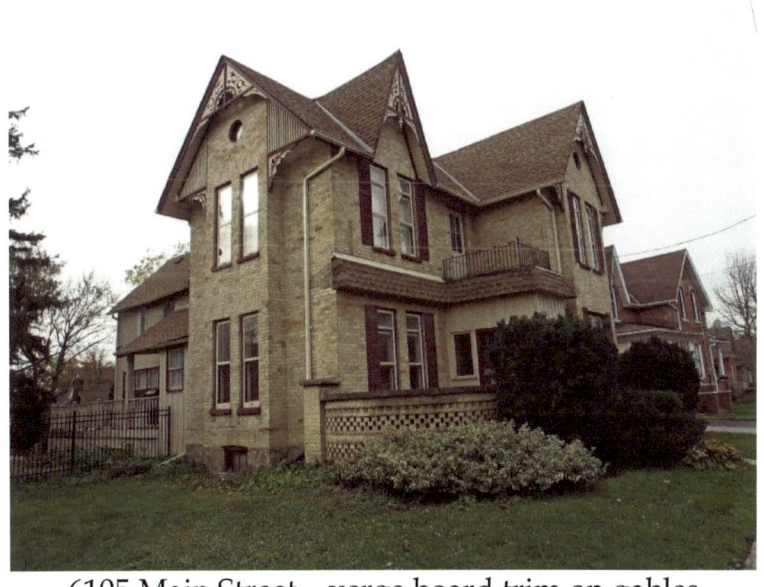

6105 Main Street – verge board trim on gables

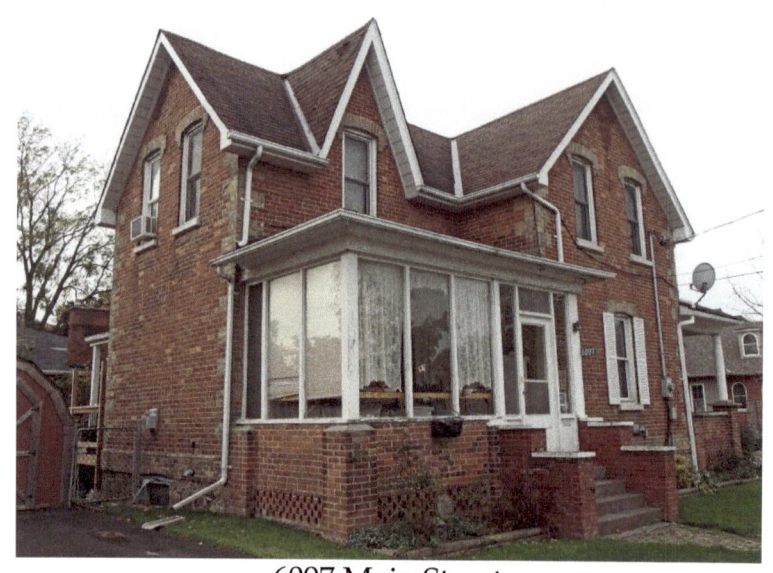

6097 Main Street

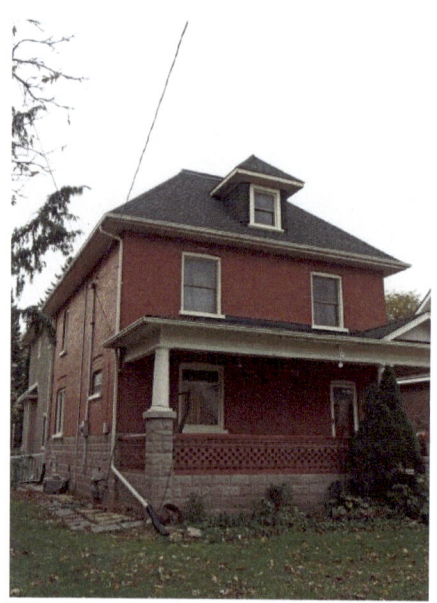

6077 Main Street – hipped roof with dormer

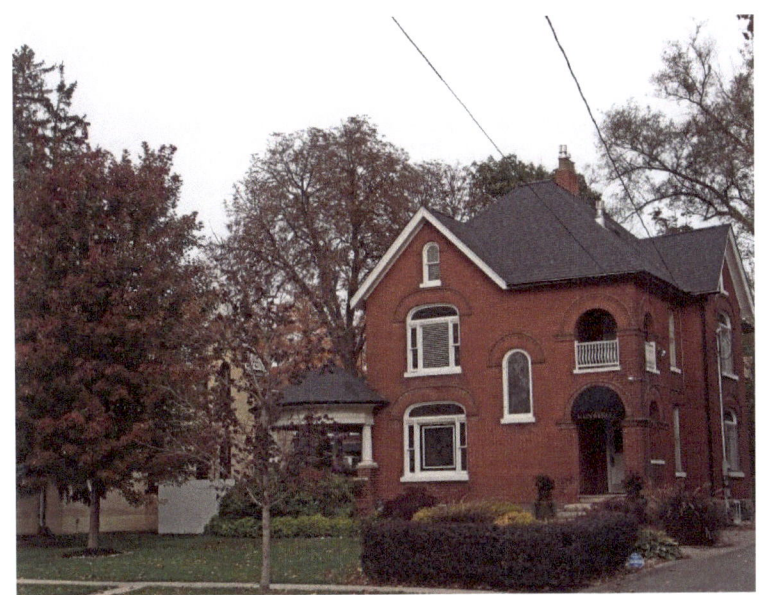

6072 Main Street

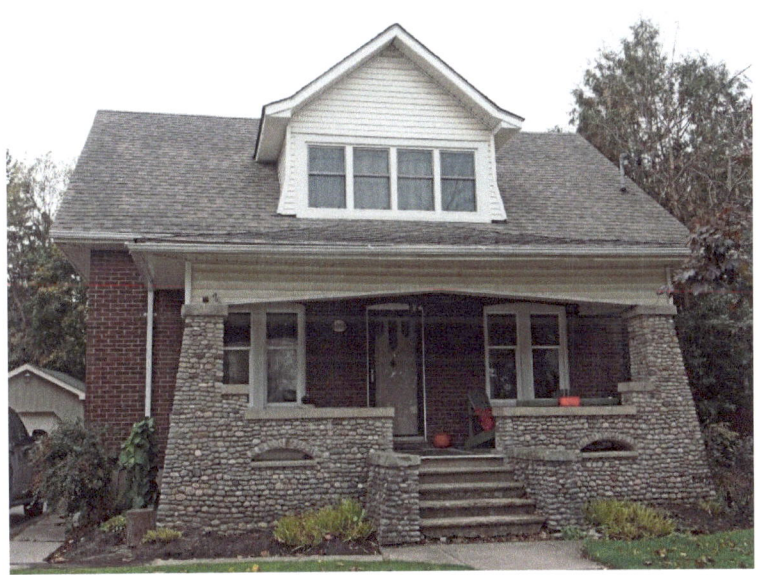

6069 Main Street – cobblestone veranda and pillars, large dormer in attic

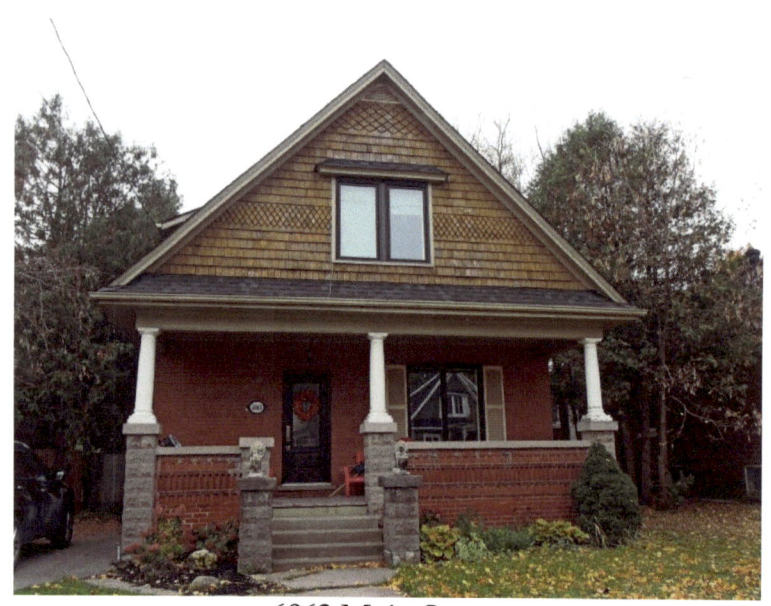

6063 Main Street

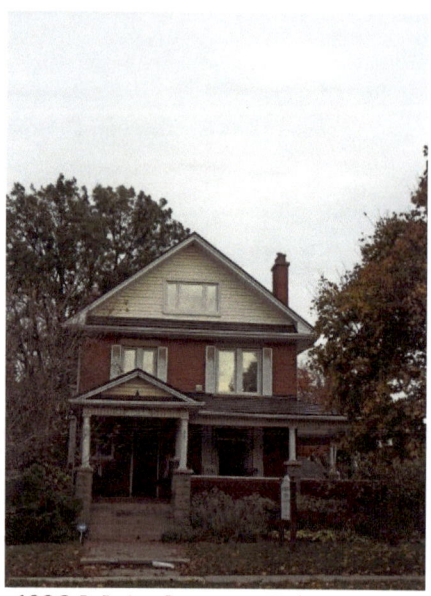

6038 Main Street - Edwardian

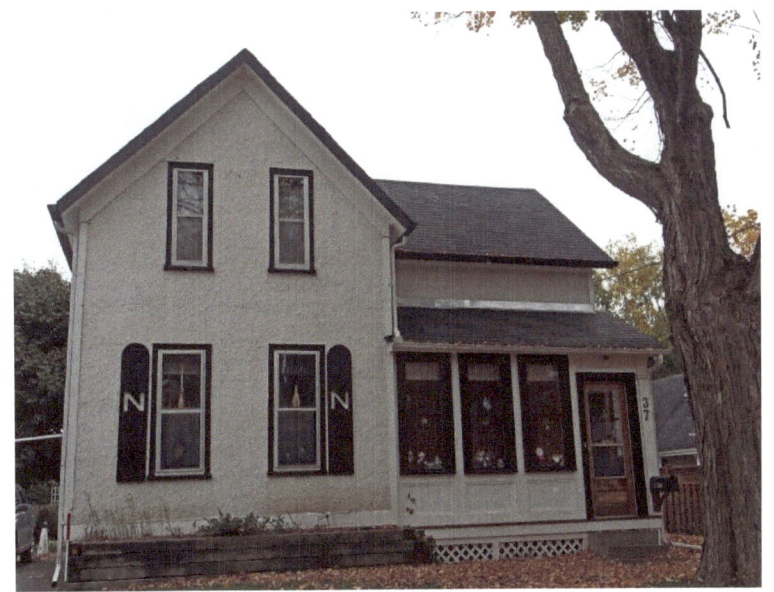

37 Charles Street – 1887 – Late Victorian Hybrid – "N" cut outs in the shutters represent the owner Nigh (2011).

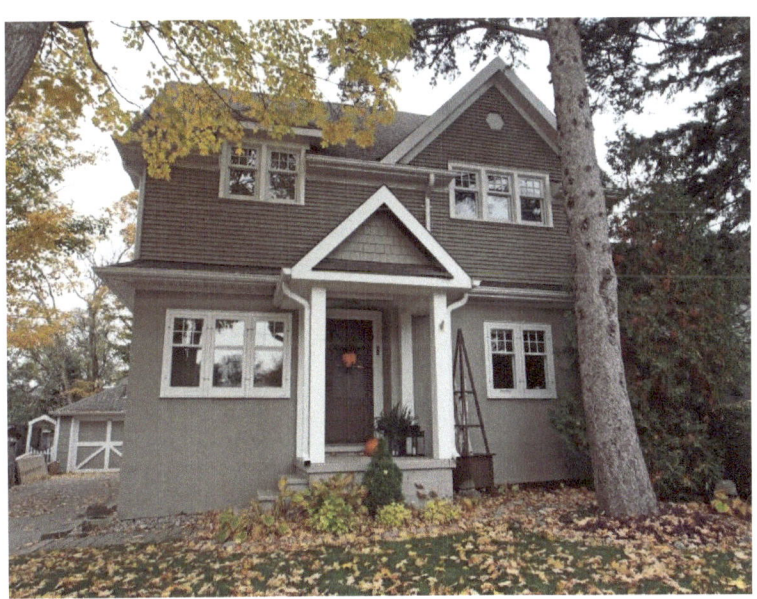

44 Charles Street

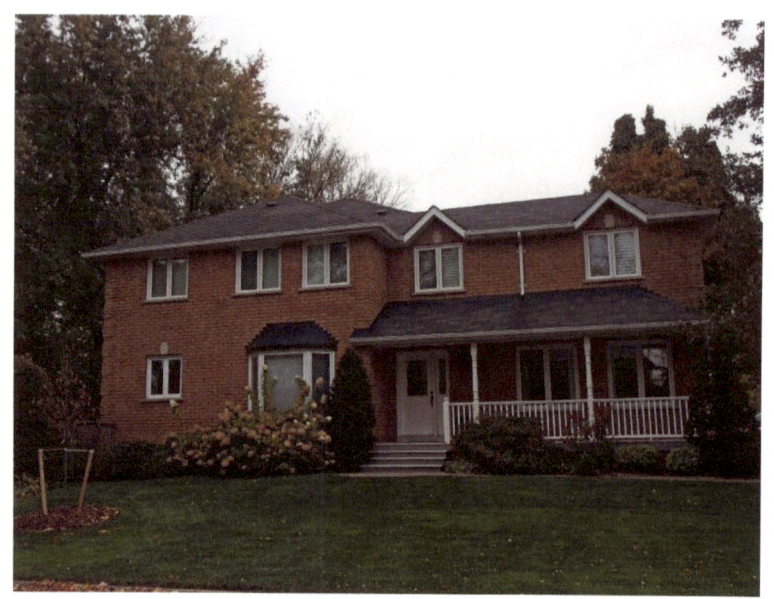

Charles Street

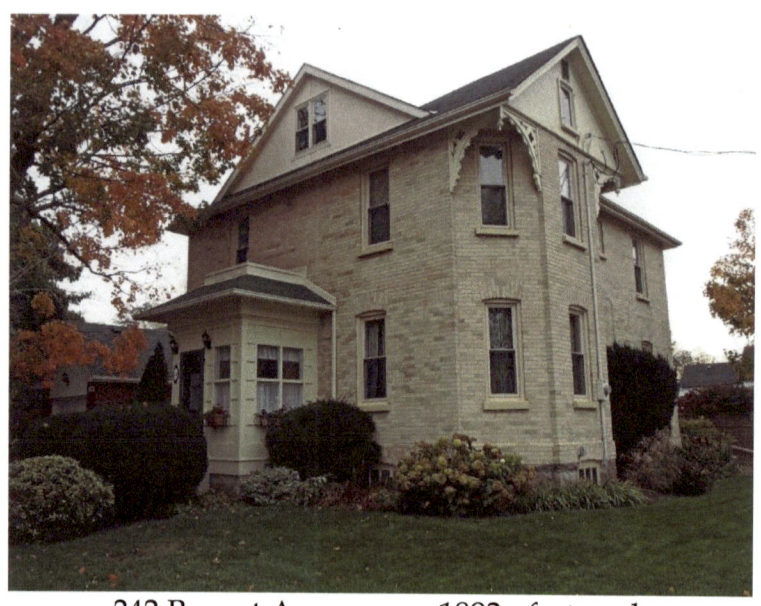

242 Rupert Avenue – c. 1892 - fretwork

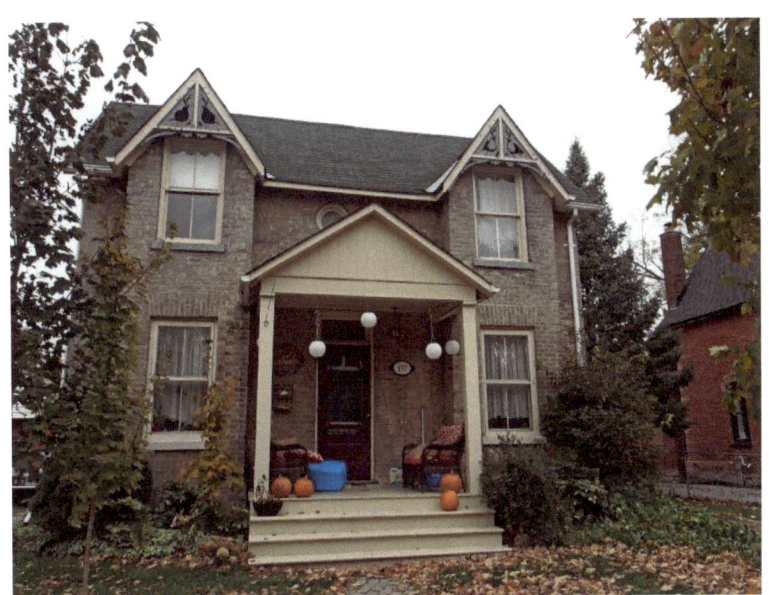

197 Rupert Avenue

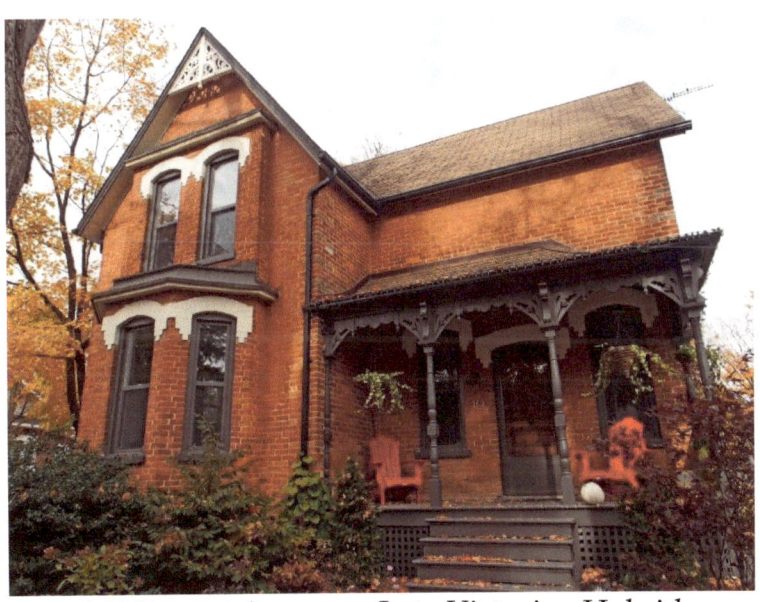

169 Rupert Avenue – Late Victorian Hybrid

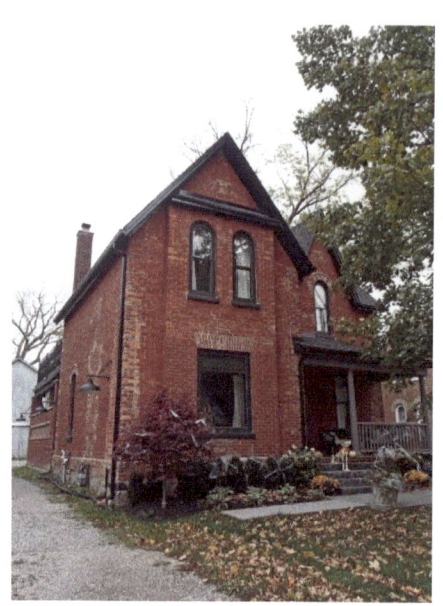

Rupert Avenue

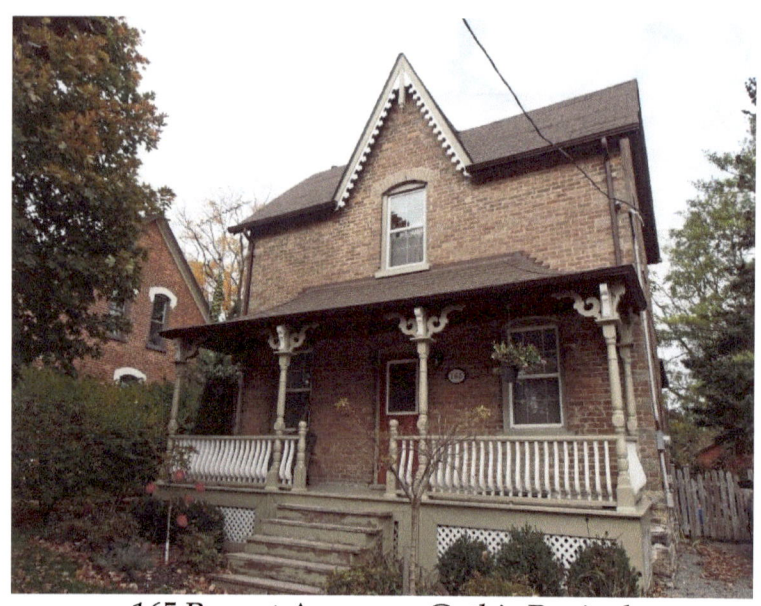

165 Rupert Avenue – Gothic Revival

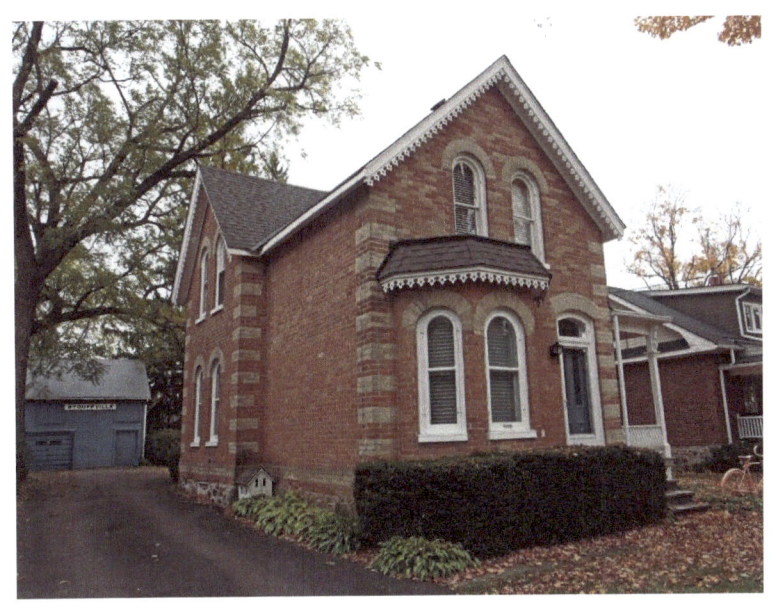

185 Rupert Avenue – Late Victorian Hybrid – quoins, bay window

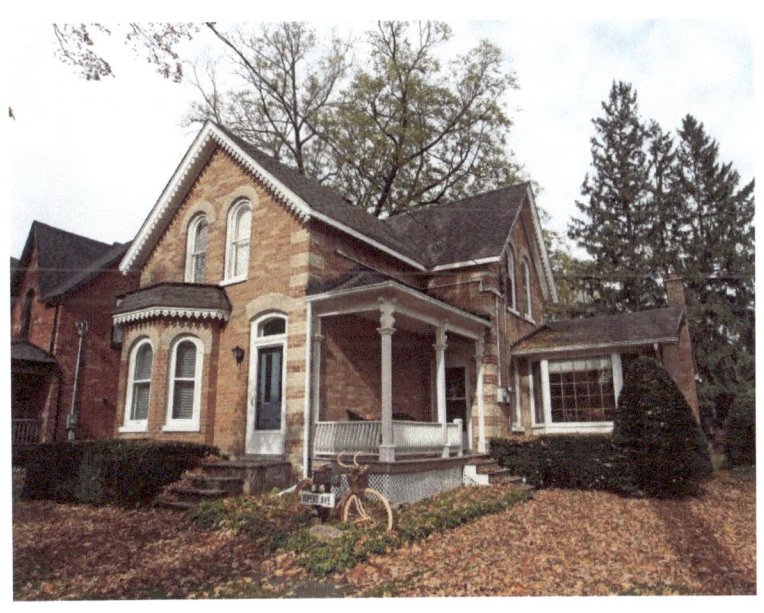

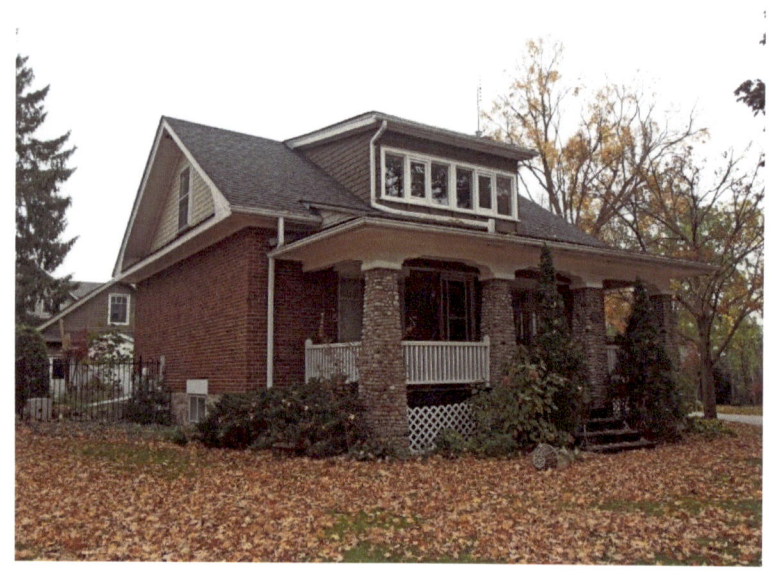

179 Rupert Avenue – shed dormer – cobblestone porch pillars

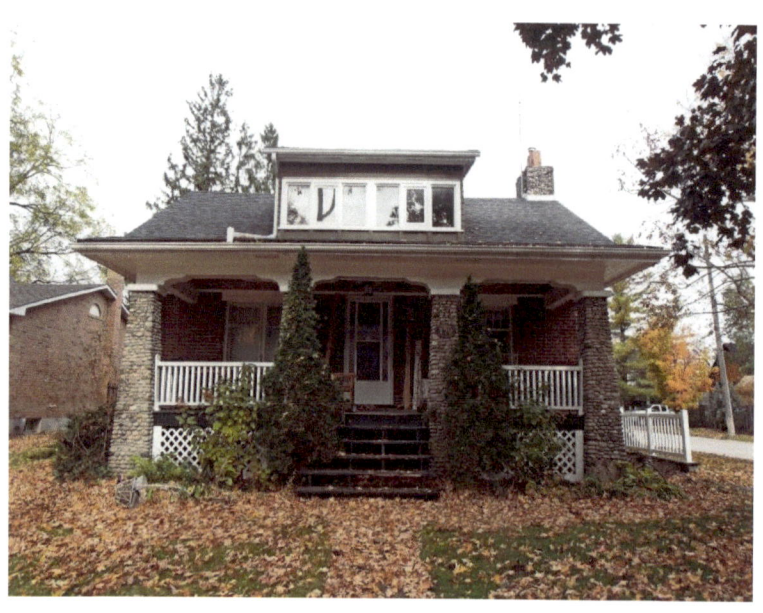

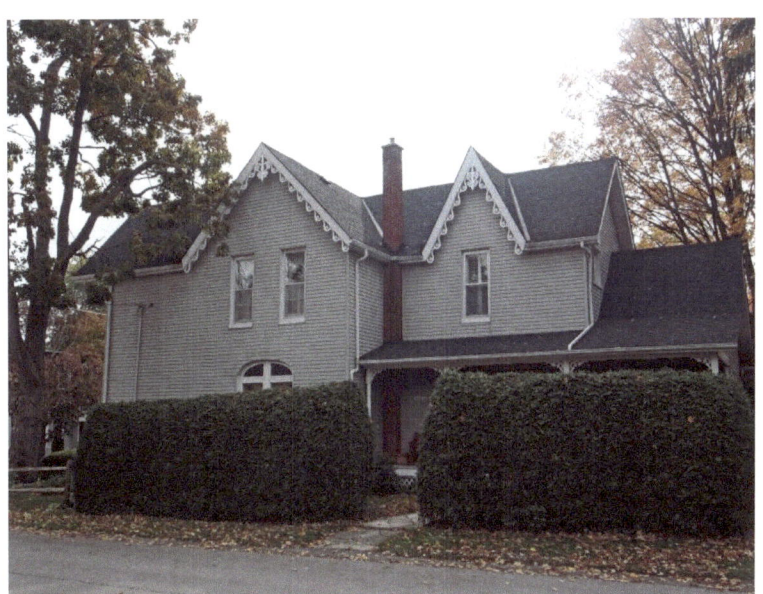

Rupert Avenue

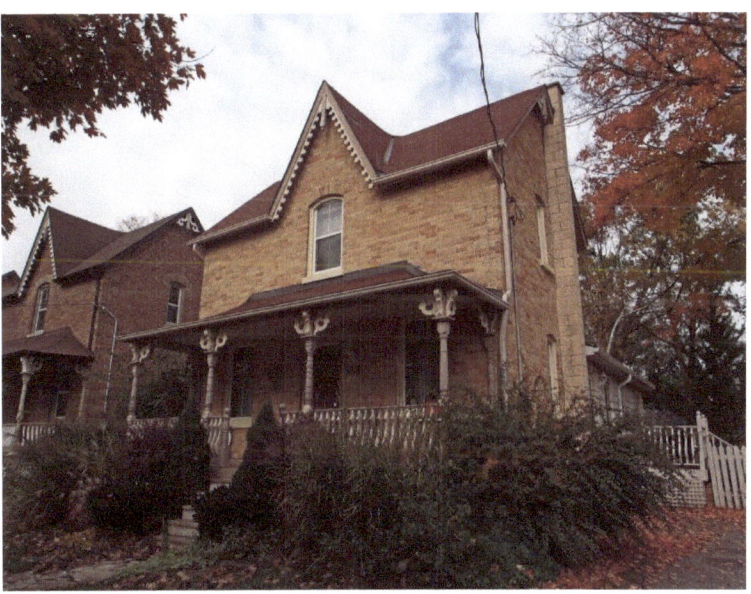

155 Rupert Avenue – Gothic Revival

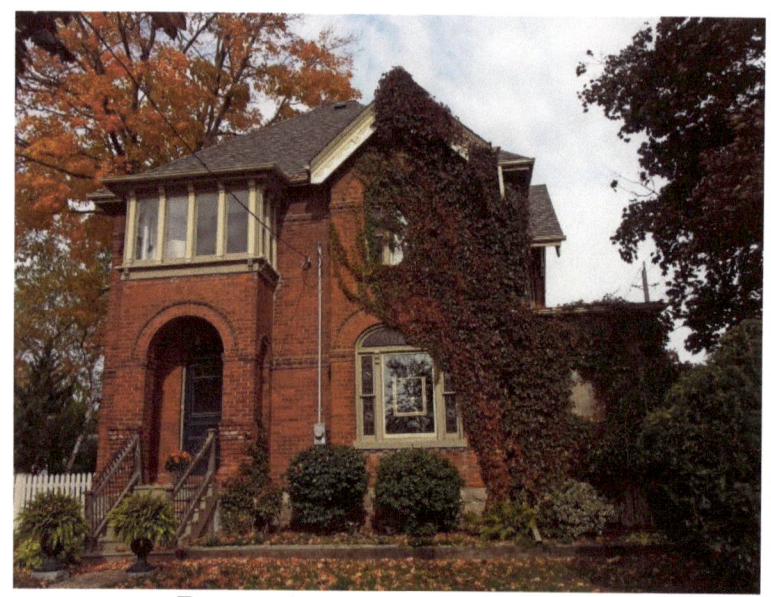

Rupert Avenue - Romanesque

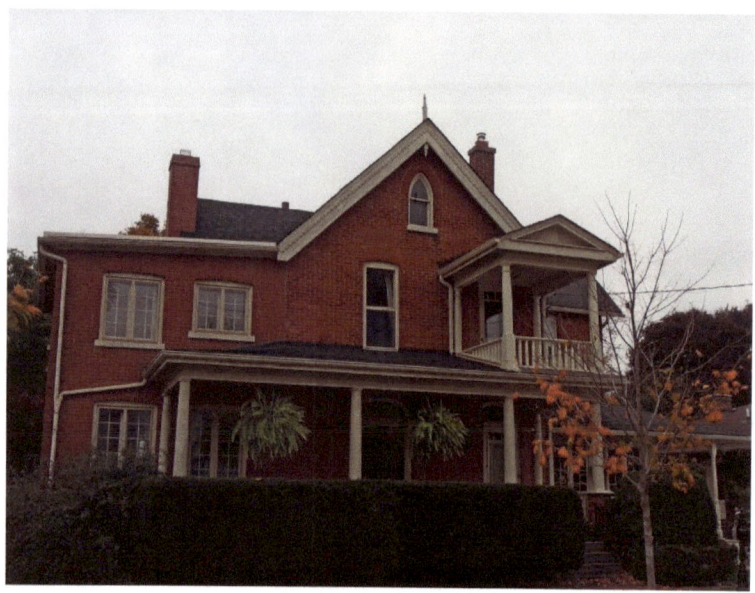

William Street

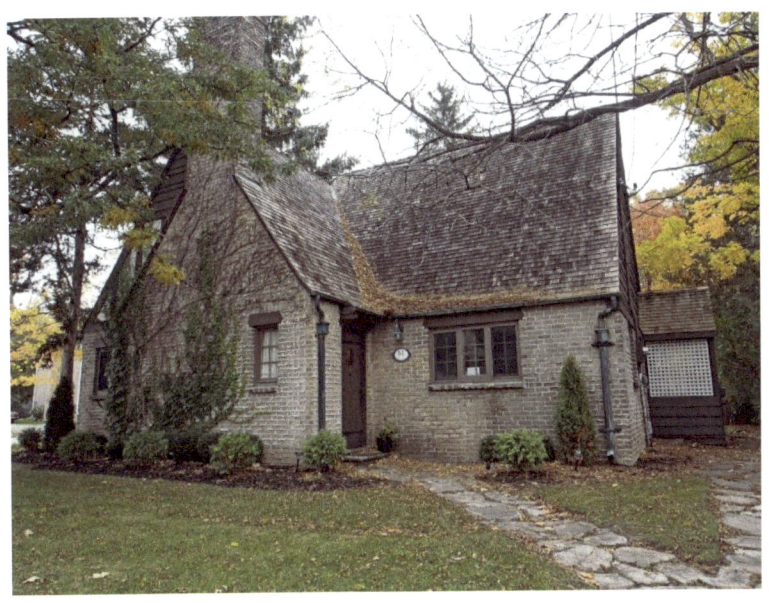

51 William Street

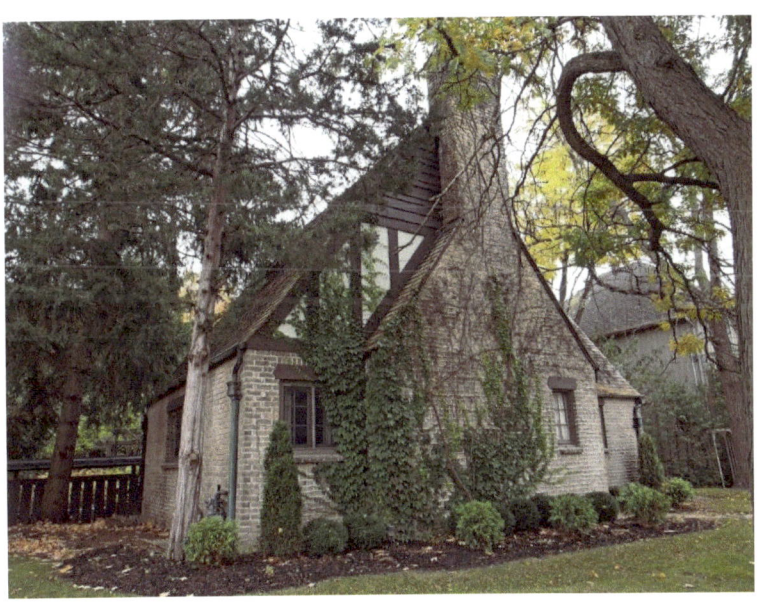

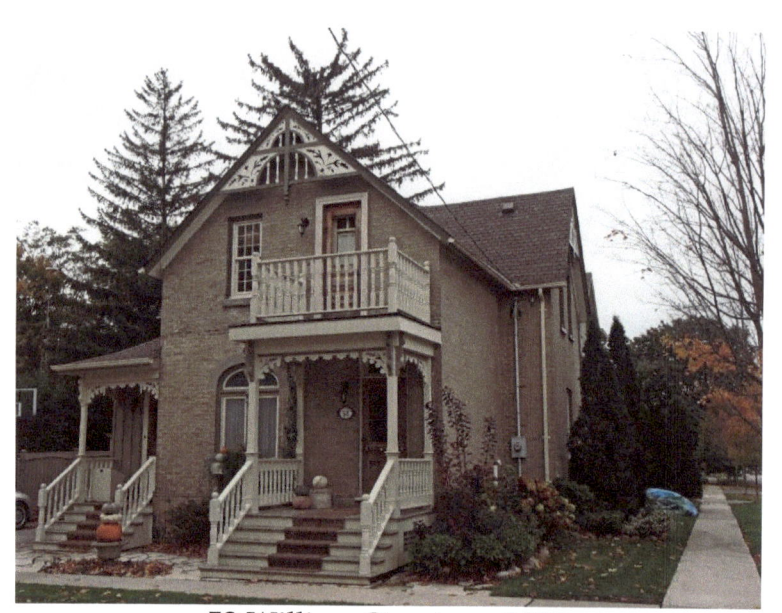

52 William Street – c. 1892

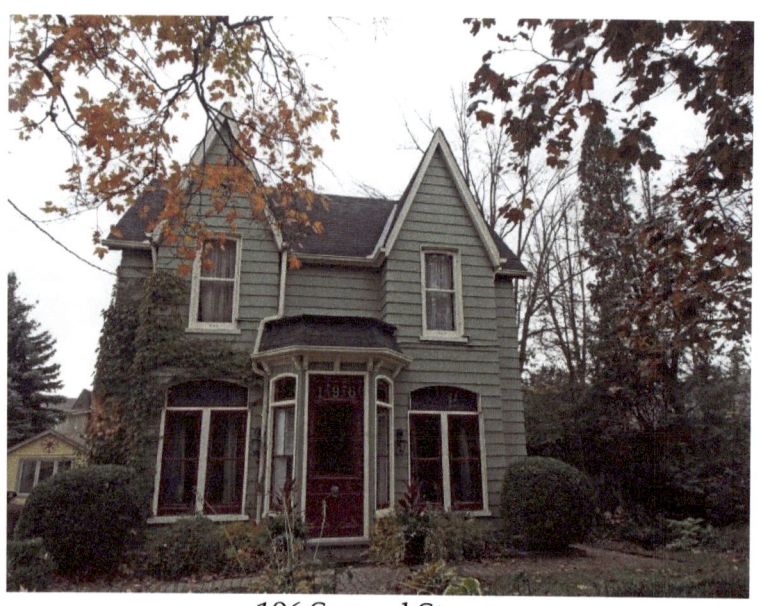

196 Second Street

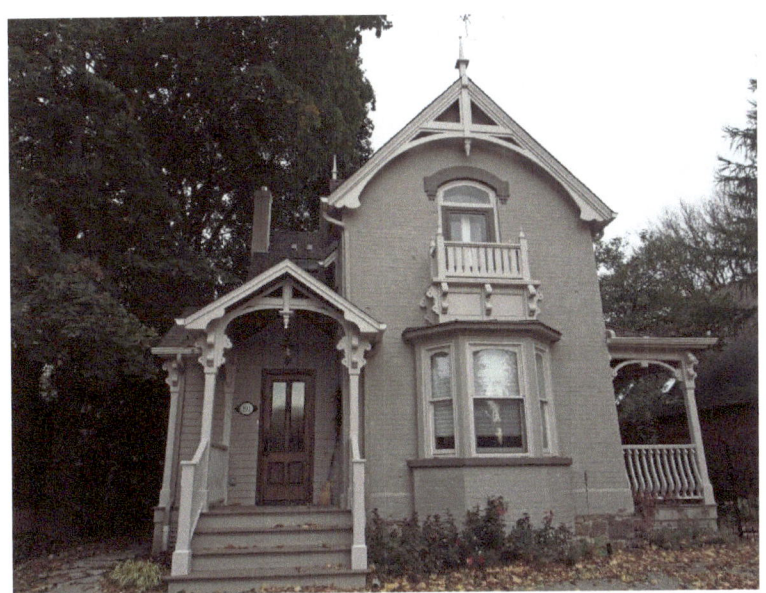

191 Second Street

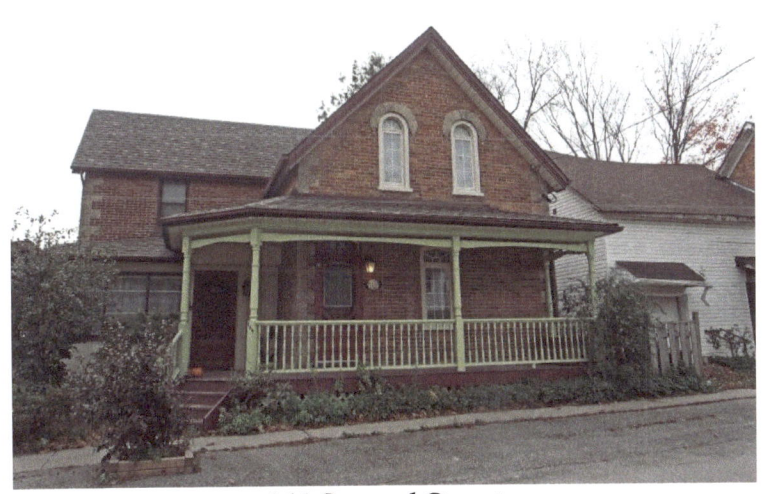

164 Second Street

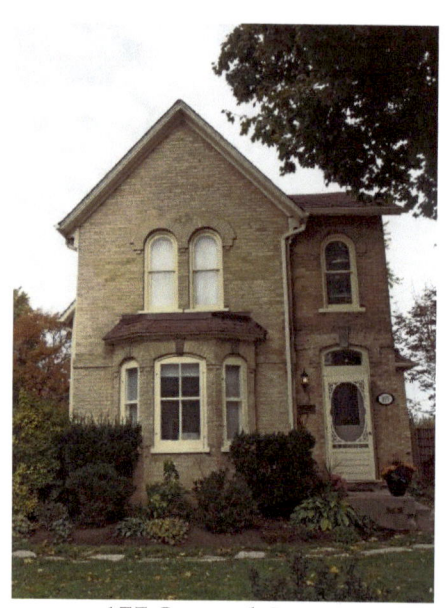

155 Second Street

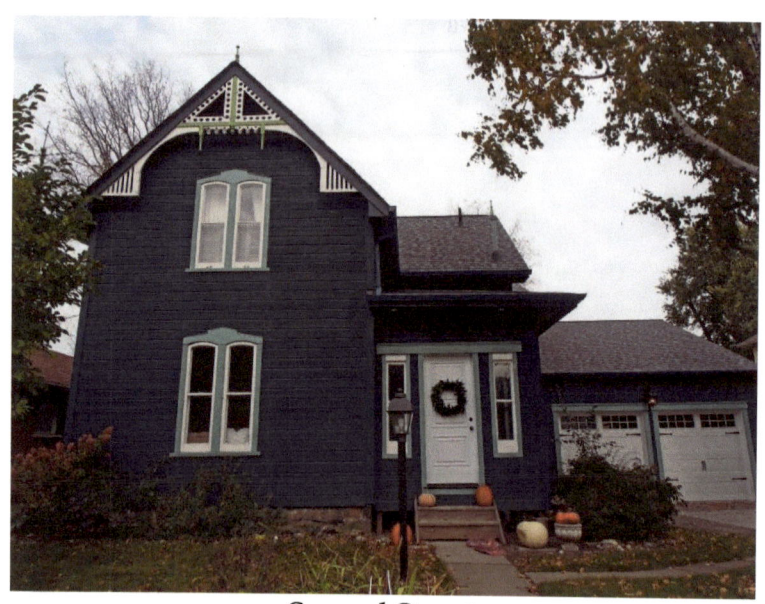

Second Street

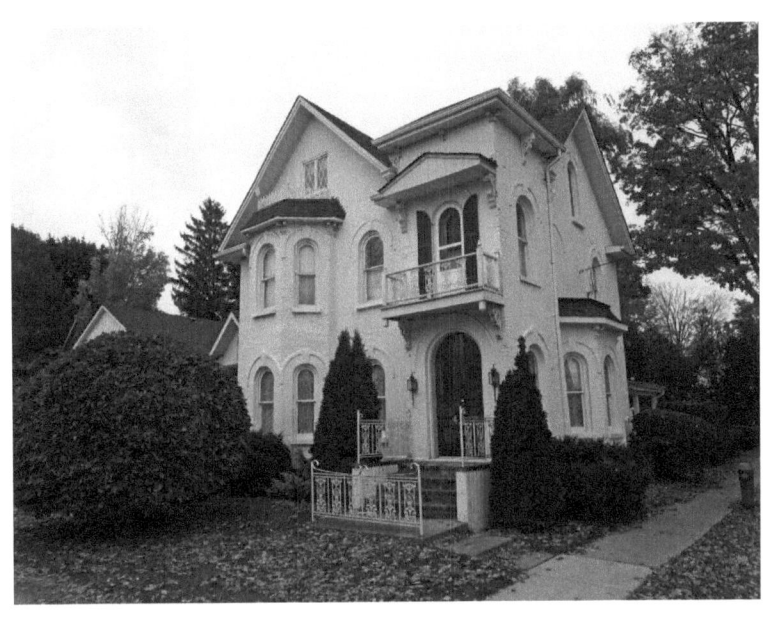

30 Albert Street – Italianate Villa – 1884 – It has a rare original semi-circular wood door.

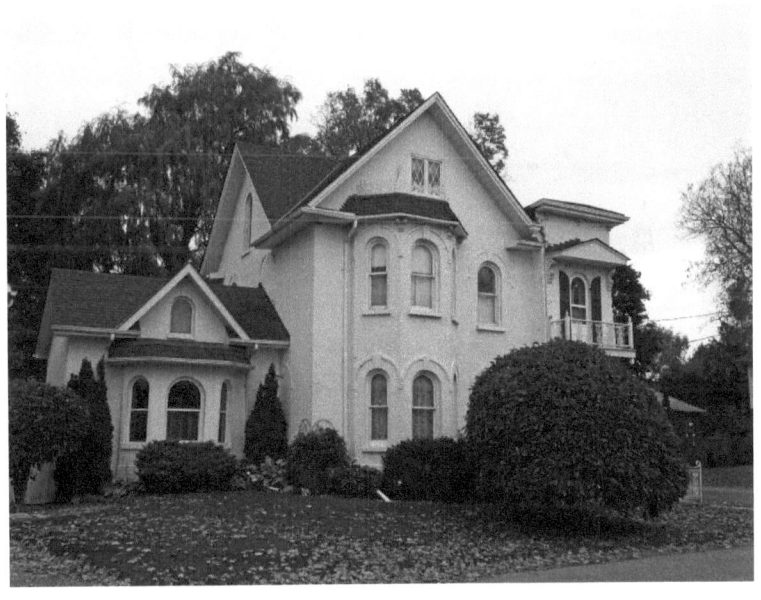

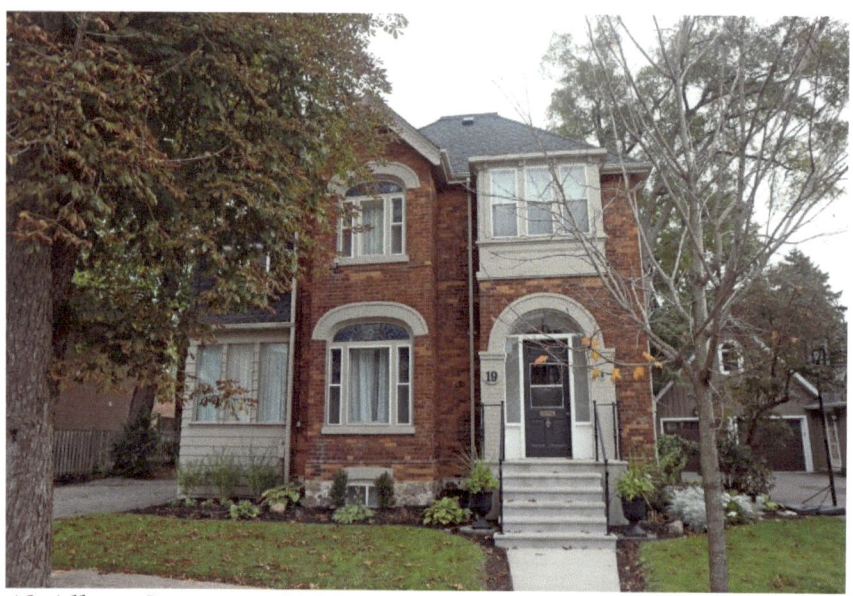

19 Albert Street – c. 1896 – Romanesque/Queen Anne – built for Joseph A. Todd, owner of the Todd block; he was a dealer in grain, flour, feed, coal, wood, seeds, potatoes, pork, corn, beans, felt roofing, salt in barrels, bulk lime, cement, plaster, fire brick, tile, wood, etc. He operated grain elevators at the train station and had his office in the corner store of the block on Main Street between Edward and Albert Streets.

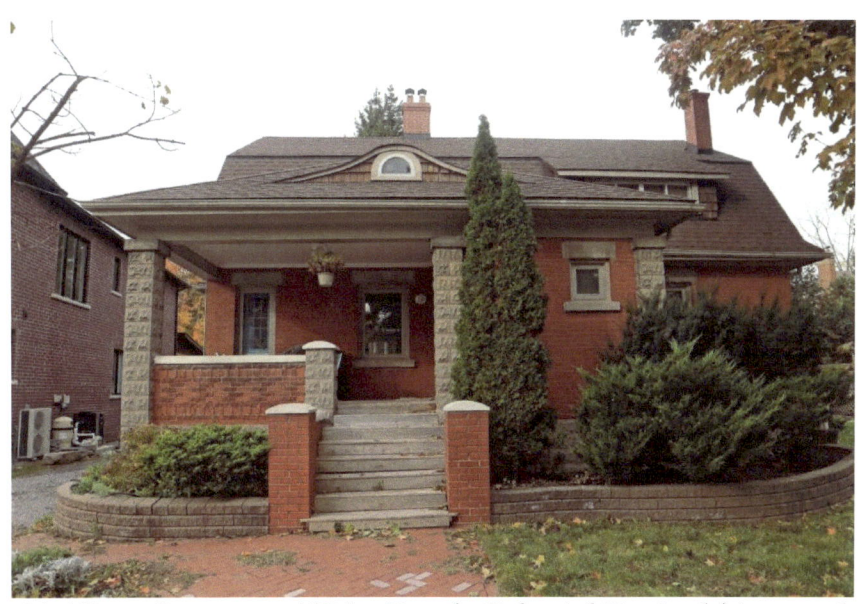

14 Albert Street – c. 1924 – Dutch Colonial Revival/Arts and Crafts architecture – eyebrow window

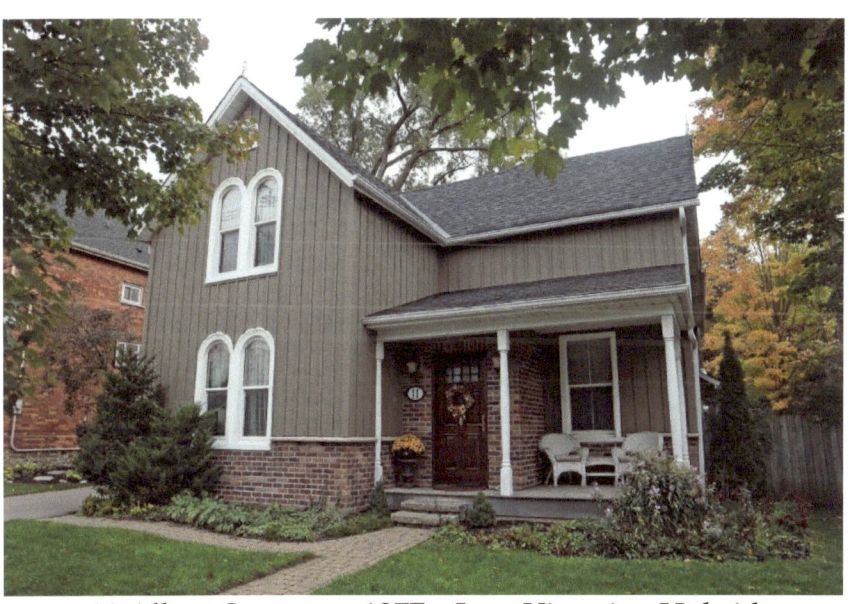

11 Albert Street – c. 1877 – Late Victorian Hybrid

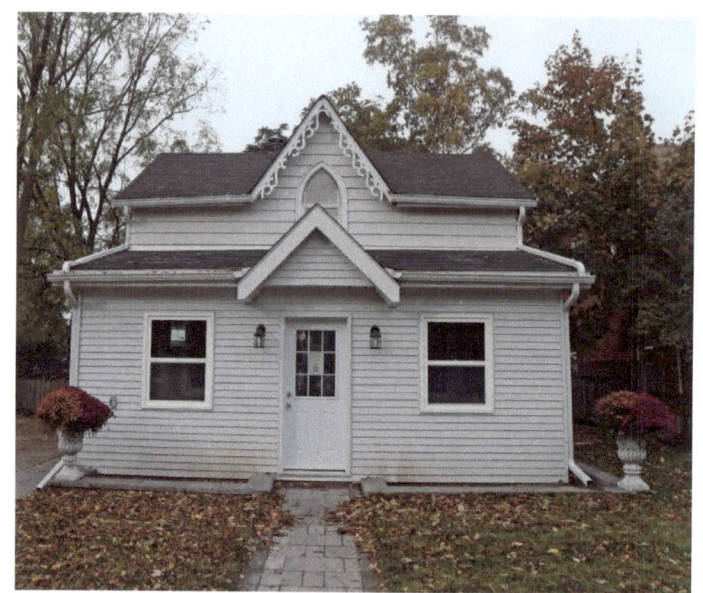

10 Albert Street – 1873 – Gothic Revival

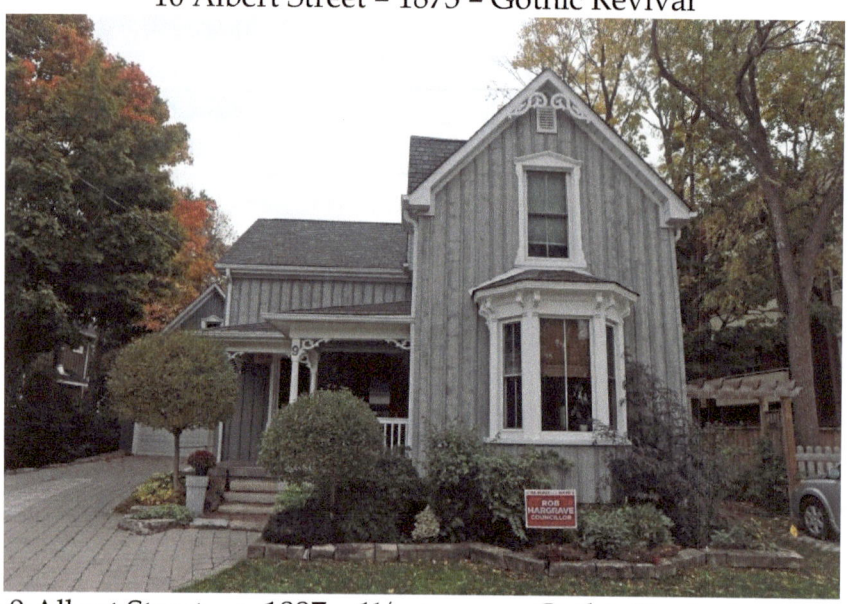

9 Albert Street – c. 1887 – 1½ storeys – Gothic Revival – John Park, co-owner of the planning mill which is now Schnell Lumber built this house for himself.

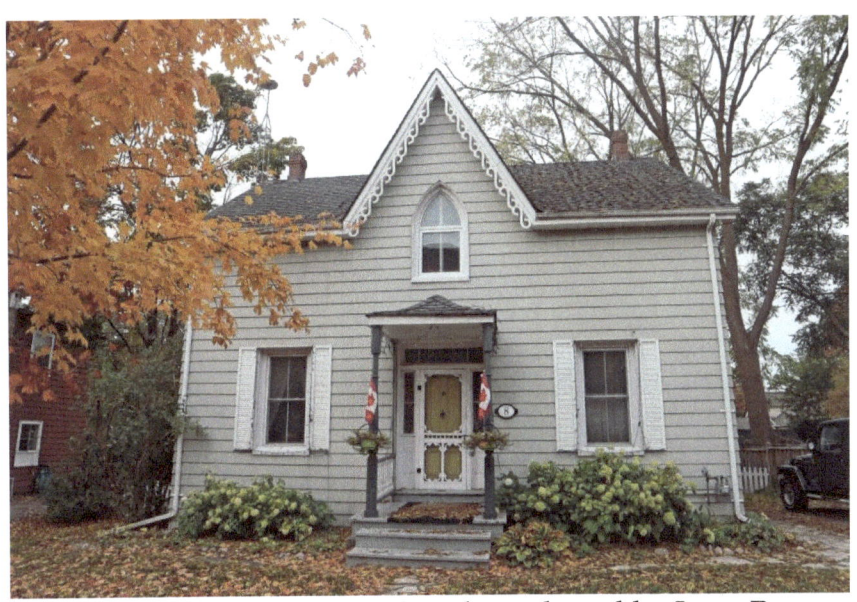

8 Albert Street – Built in 1872 and purchased by Jesse Reesor, owner of the flour mill across the street – Gothic Revival

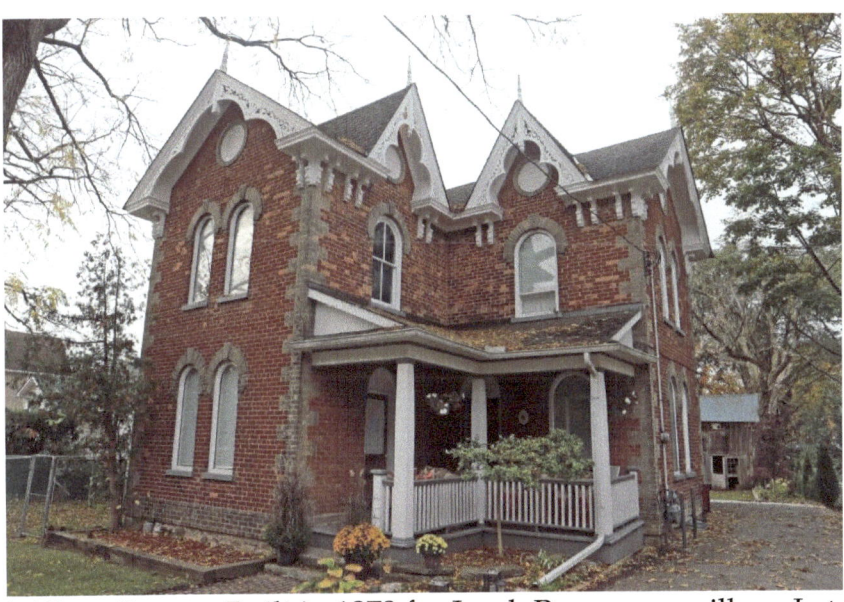

6 Albert Street – Built in 1878 for Jacob Raymer, a miller – Late Victorian hybrid with Italianate features

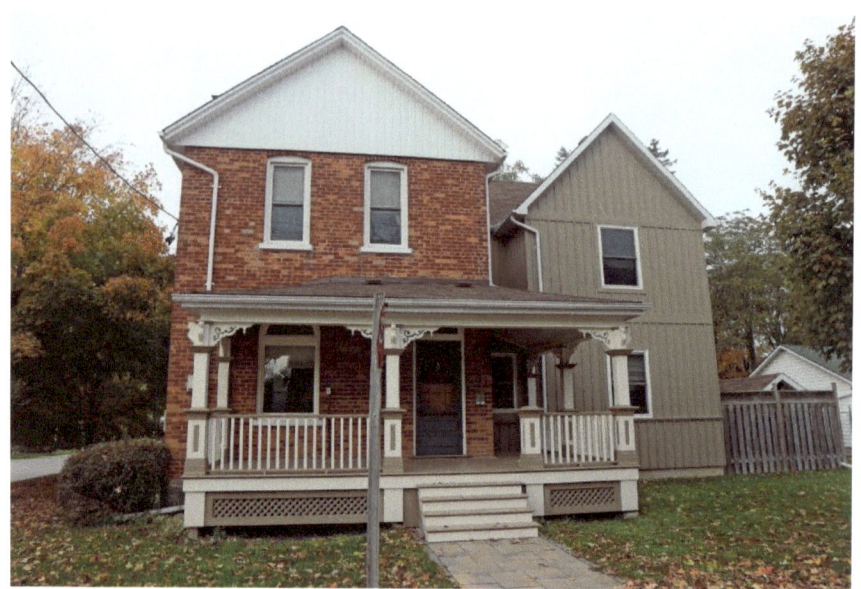

2 Albert Street – Built c. 1895 for James McConnachie, the Manager of the Toronto Fruit and Vinegar Works – two storeys, Edwardian style (board and batten addition)

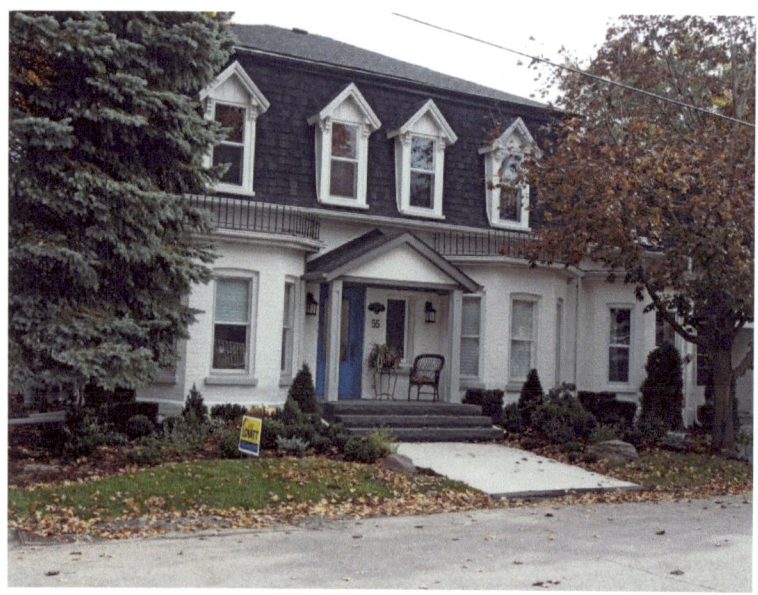

55 Albert Street

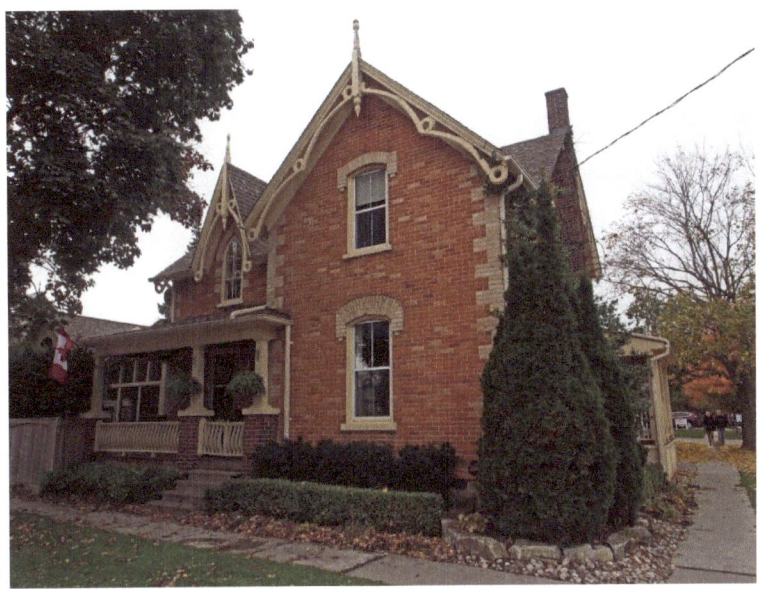

Albert Street – Late Victorian Hybrid – finials, verge board trim, corner quoins

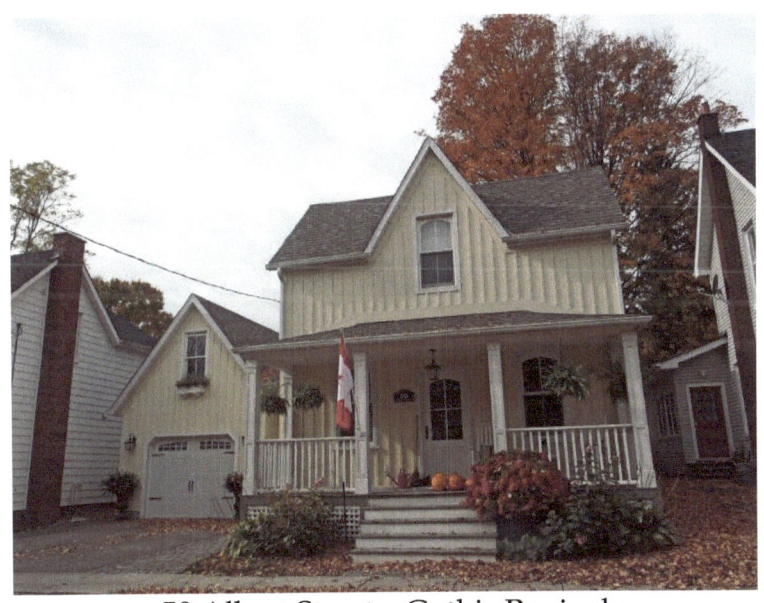

50 Albert Street – Gothic Revival

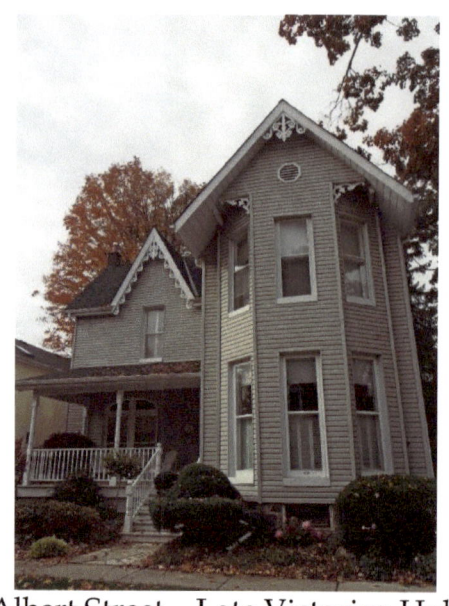

54 Albert Street – Late Victorian Hybrid

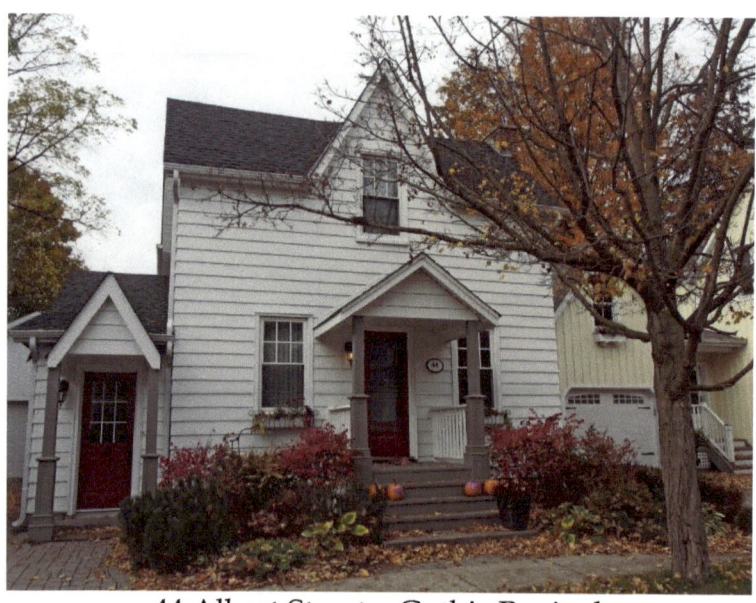

44 Albert Street – Gothic Revival

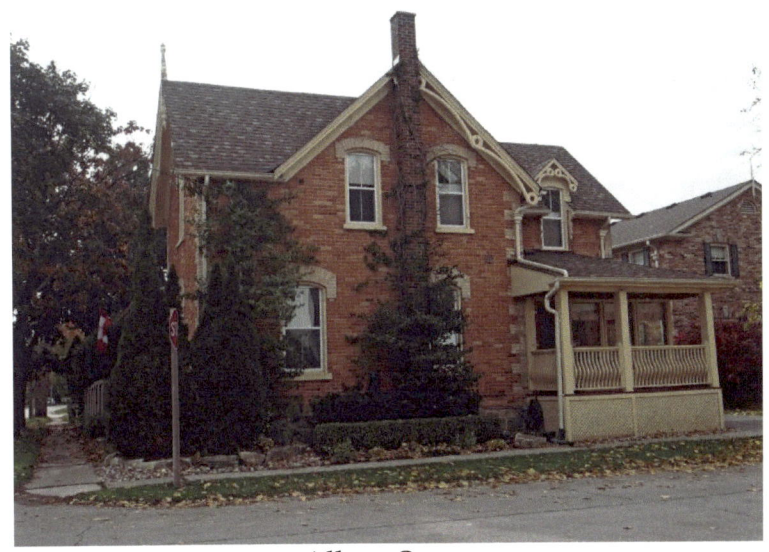

Albert Street

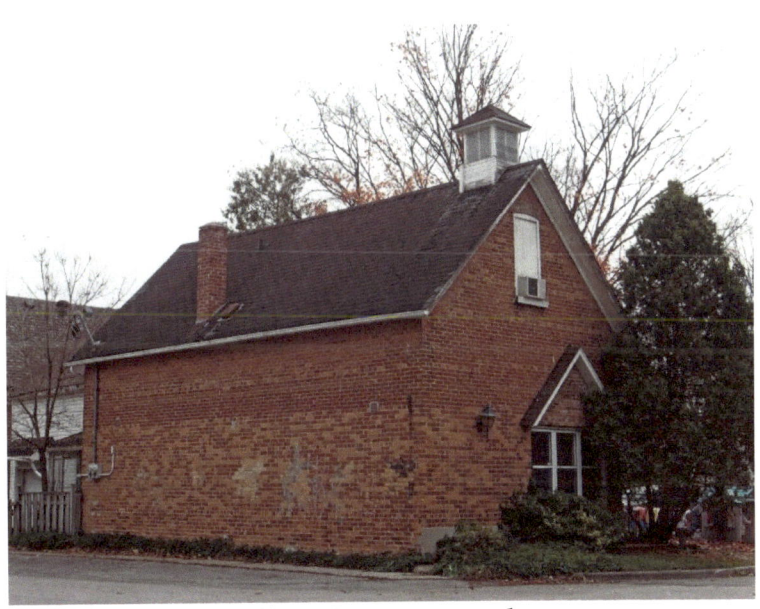

Albert Street – cupola

Building Styles

Arts and Crafts: The overlying theme - the house was based on the function of the house. Rooms were oriented to take advantage of the movement of the sun for warmth and light during daylight hours. Side entrances allowed for useable space on the front facade for light or garden use. Arts and Crafts houses have many of these features: wood, stone or stucco siding; low-pitched roof; wide eaves with triangular brackets; exposed roof rafters; porch with thick square or round columns; stone porch supports; exterior chimney made with stone; open floor plans with few hallways; many windows, some with stained or leaded glass; beamed ceilings; dark wood wainscoting and moldings; built-in cabinets, shelves, and seating.

Dutch Colonial Revival, 1890-1930 - is distinguished by its gambrel roof, with or without flared eaves, and the frequent use of dormers. The gambrel style allowed an almost complete second floor without the expense of two-story construction. Characteristics: 1½ to 2 storeys, clapboard or shingle siding, usually symmetrical facades, gable-end chimneys, round windows in gable end, porch under overhanging eaves, shed, hipped or gable dormers, columns for porches and entry.

Edwardian, 1900-1930 – This style bridges the ornate and elaborate styles of the Victorian era and the simplified styles of the 20th century. Edwardian Classicism provided simple, balanced facades, simple rooflines, dormer windows, large front porches, and smooth brick surfaces. Voussoirs and keystones are used sparingly and are understated. Finials and cresting are absent. Cornice brackets and braces are block-like and openings have flat arches or plain stone lintels.

Gothic Revival, 1830-1890 – These decorative buildings have sharply-pitched gables with highly detailed verge boards, pointed-arch window openings, and dichromatic brickwork. It is a common style in Ontario.

Italianate, 1850-1900 – A two story rectangular building with a mild hip roof, a projecting frontispiece, and generous eaves with ornate cornice brackets was the basis of the style; often there are large sash windows, quoins, ornate detailing on the windows, belvederes and wraparound verandahs. Italianate commercial buildings often have cast iron cresting and elegant window surrounds.

Italian Villa: This style was the first Ontario style that broke from the architectural traditions of the first settlers and imitated the harmony and balance of Classical architecture found in Northern Italian villas. The style is strictly residential and is characterized by an irregular roofline punctuated by a tall tower or campanile (bell tower). Small balconies, cantilevered eaves offering deep summer shade and arcaded porticos are standard features. Architects designing these houses were clearly after the picturesque.

Neo-colonial architecture seeks to revive elements of architectural style of American colonial architecture of the period around the Revolutionary War which drew strongly from Georgian architecture of Great Britain. Architecture from the 18th and early 19th centuries in Ontario includes a wide assortment of detailing and ornament applied to a design centered around the fireplace and the source of water. Structures are typically two stories, have a symmetrical front facade with elaborate front doorways, often with decorative crown pediments, fanlights, and sidelights, symmetrical windows flanking the front entrance, often in pairs or threes, and columned porches.

Ontario Cottage - one or one-and-a-half story buildings with a cottage or hip roof. The cottage roof is an equal hip roof where each hip extends to a point in the center of the roof. The hip roof has a long hip in the center. The Ontario Cottage is the vernacular design of the Regency Cottage which generally has a more ornate doorway and a partial or full verandah surrounding it. The roof can have a dormer, a belvedere, and generally two chimneys.

Queen Anne, 1885-1900 – This style is distinguished by an irregular outline featuring a combination of an offset tower, broad gables, projecting two-storey bays, verandahs, multi-sloped roofs, and tall, decorative chimneys. A mixture of brick and wood is common. Windows often have one large single-paned bottom sash and small panes in the upper sash.

Romanesque Revival, 1880-1910 – This style hearkens back to medieval architecture of the 11th and 12th centuries with a heavy appearance, blocky towers and rounded arches.

Second Empire, 1860-1880 – The mansard roof is the most noteworthy feature of this style and is evidence of the French origins. Projecting central towers and one or two-storey bays can also be present.

Victorian - In Ontario, a Victorian style building can be seen as any building built between 1840 and 1900 that doesn't fit into any of the other categories. It encompasses a large group of buildings constructed in brick, stone, and timber, using an eclectic mixture of Classical and Gothic motifs.

Other Books by Barbara Raue

Coins of Gold
Arrows, Indians and Love
The Life and Times of Barbara
The Cromwell Family Book
Laura Secord Discovered
Daddy Where Are You?

Montana Series
Book 1: Montana Dream
Book 2: Life on the Montana Frontier
Book 3: Montana to Boston and Back
Book 4: Montana Sons Go to War
Book 5: Montana Sons Return from War

Visit Barbara's website to view all of her books
http://barbararaue.ca

© 2018 by Barbara Raue - All the photos in this book have been taken with my cameras. I own the rights to them.

www.ingramcontent.com/pod-product-compliance
Lightning Source LLC
Chambersburg PA
CBHW040236220526
45473CB00001B/258